Bread: A Beginners Guide

Written by: James Shipley

Edited by: Lisa Vaughn

Shipley Publishing

Shipley Publishing

www.shipleypublishing.com

Editing by Lisa Vaughn

Cover Text and Design by James Shipley and Lisa Vaughn

ISBN-13: 978-1482526332

ISBN-10: 1482526336

Contents

Preface

Writing a beginners guide to bread is a daunting task. I felt caught between two armies. The first is that of the professionals, who remind me to use only time-honored techniques, to carefully weigh ingredients, and to let time do important work.

My heroes are on the professional side. These heroes are bakers who produce magic. They write books that I find delight in every time I carefully recreate their alchemic wizardry with reverent aplomb.

Then, on the other side, I hear the cries of my friends, my family. These people do not have the experience to follow the great bread wizards. "I want bread too!", they shout, "...and I don't want to spend two days making it!"

With all of this in mind, I went to work to take many of my favorite recipes and condense the steps to the absolute essentials. I made recipes that would produce a great tasting bread with the least amount of work and without the meticulous precision that is required by professional bakers.

Many of my bread recipes can be completed in just an hour or two. For the ones that require a bit more time, there is still little active work involved in the production.

Acknowledgments

I would like to thank, first and foremost, Lisa Vaughn, my editor, fiancé, and best friend. I love you, and this project would not have been possible without your encouragement and belief.

I would like to thank all the people who believed in this project before it became alive. You are my "kickstarter" backers, through www.kickstarter.com. If you are one of these amazing people, your book is signed just below this paragraph. Thank you for sharing the vision for great bread to be made at home and for supporting me in bringing "Bread: A Beginners Guide" to life.

Thank you to my grandmother, Genevieve Raschick, an amazing cook, baker, and role model. May you rest in peace.

Finally, thank you to Eowynn, my puppy of 8 1/2 years. Eowynn is who sits beside me for every moment of writing and baking, who gets me outside for walks, and who is always my biggest fan.

James Shipley

Introduction

Welcome to Bread: A Beginners Guide!

Bread is universal. The goal of this book is to give you quick success in bread making for a variety of breads, many with international roots. I want your global food knowledge to grow in this area of breads, as it is fun and easy to pair new types of breads with your normal meals to make "fusion" meals. You can be creative with many of my recipes, such as making my naan recipe, then make it into garlic bread to serve with your spaghetti.

Before you begin making recipes, please read over the informational sections as there are important details found there to guide you to bread awesomeness. For example, I discuss ingredients in a section to help you read and measure for each recipe. Ingredient information will also make the aisles at the store less confusing for purchases.

I do not use machines, as I would prefer that everything be done by hand. I do include instructions for mixers as an alternative but do not discuss bread machines.

Why by hand? I want you to feel the bread changing as you work with it. You will feel the ingredients combining or "coming together". You will feel the bread beginning to "push back". You will learn to recognize by sight and smell when a dough has had enough time to ferment, and you will recognize the difference from a cold or warm ferment.

I do not use weight measurements for the ingredients in this book. Instead, I use volume measurements and for a very specific reason: I want this book to be accessible, to be comfy. Professional bread recipes use only weight, but understand that even weight measurement recipes depend on conditions like humidity, ingredient quality, elevation, temperature, and the individual baker. Using weight does not guarantee accuracy. Using careful volume measurements that I explain in the ingredients section will make you accurate enough for the recipes I have designed for you as a beginner.

The recipes in this book have been streamlined to be as quick as possible. I do this to make bread-baking less intimidating and to make it fit within any busy lifestyle. That is not to say that the longer, professional-style recipes are without merit, as those lengthy processes usually deliver an excellent product that has a greater depth of taste than a shorter time will allow. What I have found is that many types of great breads can be made within a short time and can be duplicated by a home baker.

After you have taken the time to bake your way through many of these recipes and feel more confident about your beginner level bread-making skills, I encourage you to try some of the more involved preparations in professional books and compare results.

Ingredients

...& How to Measure Each

Measuring Tip: Any time you are measuring and have a heaping amount to level off, place a plate, bowl, or similar item under your measuring work area to catch the excess that you level off. The excess can be returned to the original container to eliminate a waste of ingredients.

Baking Powder and Baking Soda:

Make sure these are no more than six months old! If these are not fresh, these will not work as effectively.

Measure these by scooping a heaping amount out of the container with the appropriate size measuring spoon, then use a flat edge (like a table knife) to remove the excess, leaving a smooth, leveled amount for an exact measurement.

Bakers outside the US, please reference the conversion chart.

Flour:

There are many types of flour available in grocery markets. I want to clarify the difference between three of the major flours to avoid confusion when you purchase your flours.

First, there is pastry flour, which is also called cake flour. We will not be using this flour for recipes in this book, and it is not an acceptable substitute. It contains too little gluten to be useful in the creation of bread.

Second, there is AP or All-Purpose flour. It is between a very low-gluten pastry flour and high-gluten bread flour. For baking, AP can be used in pastry recipes and may be used in some making bread recipes. If AP will work in a recipe, then I will specify that choice. Otherwise, know that AP can be substituted for bread flour in general on some occasions, but AP will require a significantly longer amount of kneading time to develop the structure required for hearty style breads.

Third, bread flour is the main type of flour used in this book. It can also be called high-gluten flour, because its defining feature is its high gluten content, which provides the structure necessary for making great bread.

Flours are broken down further by their source, such as whole wheat, rye, sunflower, rice, etc.

When purchasing flour for a recipe, check for both the type of flour and the source of the flour to get the correct one.

Measure by putting the appropriate sized measuring cup on a flat surface, then pour the flour from its original container into the cup until it is heaping. Then, use a flat edge (like a table knife) to remove the excess, leaving a smooth, leveled amount for an exact measurement. Do NOT scoop the flour from the container, as this can compact/pack the floor and end up measuring too much. Do NOT shake the measuring cup to level off the flour, this may also result in settling/packing of flour and end up measuring too much.

Bakers outside the US, please reference the conversion chart.

Eggs:

Check eggs for stamped expiration date first. Then, check the freshness by cracking one egg onto a plate, noting that if the two parts stay close together, then the egg is fresh. The farther the two parts spread apart, the older the egg is. Fresh eggs are vital for the baking process to be successful.

Cracking an egg: Hold the egg gently in one hand, exposing a "side" of the egg, then use a flat surface, **not an edge**, to tap lightly once, on one side of the egg. Next, hold the egg over a bowl, place the tips of your thumbs into the indent/break in the shell, and in a combined motion, pull the shell apart and upwards, allowing the entire egg contents to drop into the bowl. Toss the shell into the trash bin. Repeat for remaining needed eggs. Wash hands before moving on, as the shell is where salmonella and other "baddies" live.

Always crack eggs into a separate bowl before adding into a bowl with other ingredients. In case you have a "bad" one, you just have to replace your eggs and not all the ingredients in use up to that point.

Separating an egg: After an egg is cracked and in a bowl, cup one hand with fingers tightly closed and gently transfer the egg into that hand. Place the bowl under the cupped hand, and slightly open your fingers to allow just the "white" part to slip through and into the bowl, all the while, keeping the "yellow" yolk in your hand. Transfer the yolk into another bowl and set aside. Save the "white" part in a covered bowl in the refrigerator for other uses like breakfast eggs or in making a meringue topping.

Use "large" eggs as standard sized in US stores.

Bakers outside the US, please reference the conversion chart.

Butter:

Use unsalted butter. We can always add the exact amount of salt needed for each recipe if we know that we are starting out with a standard amount of zero salt in the butter. Check the expiration date as fresh butter is important.

Measure butter either with the "marked" 1/4 pound sticks or firmly pack butter into the appropriate size measuring cup.

Bakers outside the US, please reference the conversion chart.

Salt:

Use non-iodized Kosher or Sea salt.

Measure by scooping a heaping amount out of the container with the appropriate size measuring spoon, then use a flat edge (like a table knife) to remove the excess, leaving a smooth, leveled amount for an exact measurement.

Bakers outside the US, please reference the conversion chart.

Yeast:

Instant dried yeast is the one I use for all recipes, this is the little packets common in US grocery stores. Check the expiration date for freshness.

Yeast options are given in the conversion chart section in case you want to use a different style of yeast, all of which will work the same as the instant dried in all of my recipes.

Measure by scooping a heaping amount out of the container with the appropriate size measuring spoon, then use a flat edge (like a table knife) to remove the excess, leaving a smooth, leveled amount for an exact measurement.

Bakers outside the US, please reference the conversion chart.

Honey:

Honey changes flavor depending upon seasons, regions, and if organic, so use this ingredient to add personal preference flavors to your breads.

Before measuring honey, mist/spritz the spoon or cup with non-stick cooking oil. To measure, pour or scrape into the measuring spoon or cup until a level amount is achieved, viewing at eye level. The oil mist will release the honey into the mix much easier allowing for a more accurate measurement and for easier cleaning of the measuring device afterwards.

Bakers outside the US, please reference the conversion chart.

Sugar:

Use white, granulated sugar unless otherwise specified.

Measure these by scooping a heaping amount out of the container with the appropriate size measuring spoon / cup, then use a flat edge (like a table knife) to remove the excess, leaving a smooth, leveled amount for an exact measurement.

Bakers outside the US, please reference the conversion chart.

Warm Water:

Water should be warmed to between 80 - 100 degrees. To check this, I recommend using a thermometer. Without a thermometer, you can test it with your wrist, BUT you risk burning yourself and not having an accurate result. For the wrist method, if it the water feels comfortably warm on your wrist then it is not too warm for the yeast. If your water is too hot, then it will kill your yeast and not make your bread. Again, I recommend using a cooking thermometer now, as it can be used later in determining when bread is done, etc.

Measure warm water into appropriate size measuring cup / spoon, until a level measurement is achieved, viewing at eye level.

Bakers outside the US, please reference the conversion chart.

Milk:

Use whole bovine (cow) milk, also known as Vitamin D or full-fat, unless specified, such as heavy cream. Check the expiration date, then smell and visually inspect milk for freshness.

Measure into appropriate size measuring cup, using a flat surface for a level measurement and viewing at eye level.

Bakers outside the US, please reference the conversion chart.

Heavy Cream:

Heavy cream (bovine) can be packaged as "whipping cream".

Vanilla:

Use a PURE vanilla extract. Do NOT use artificial vanilla. When making any recipe, the product can only be as amazing as the least awesome ingredient. Vanilla extract changes flavor depending upon the region it is from, if it is organic, and how long it has aged, so use this ingredient to add personal preference flavors to your breads.

If you want to try my unique or custom vanilla extracts, then contact me for what I have available for purchase through my business as www.twobearschocolates.com.

Measure vanilla into appropriate size measuring cup / spoon, until a level measurement is achieved, viewing at eye level.

Bakers outside the US, please reference the conversion chart.

Juicing an Orange / Lemon:

Rinse the fruit under cold water and dry it. Roll the whole fruit around on a clean table, using the palm of your hand, with firm pressure. Transfer fruit to a cutting board, then use a knife to cut the fruit in half "going around the middle" (**not** going through the "navel" or the stem / nub). Set aside. Place a mesh strainer over a bowl. With bare hands, squeeze the fruit half over the strainer, as this allows the pulp and membranes to be kept out of the juice and transfer to the trash bin. Juiced citrus can be kept in the bowl, covered with plastic wrap / film for up to 3 days.

Zesting an Orange / Lemon:

If you do not have a micro-plane or zester tool, then you can use a vegetable / potato peeler or a carrot / cheese grater tool. Rinse the fruit under cold water and dry it with a clean towel. Then, with a tool, remove just the orange / yellow outermost layer of the fruit, being careful to not remove the white layer underneath. The white layer is the pith (rhymes with "with") and is bitter. Remove all of the colored layer. If you used a micro-plane or zester, then you are done. If you used an alternate tool, then transfer peelings / gratings to a cutting board and use a knife to mince. "Finely minced zest" is about the same size as coarse sea salt. Keep the fruit without its peel in a plastic sealable bag for up to 1 week.

Candied Ginger:

Candied ginger is normally sold near dried fruits. There will be many pieces in a plastic container. These mince best if you place one piece at a time on the cutting board. Then, with a sharp knife, slice lengthwise, in super thin strips all the way across. Turn the board 90 degrees, then cut in super thin pieces until all strips are minced.

Measure the minced bits in a measuring spoon of appropriate size, loosely placed.

In General:

I recommend organic products whenever available, and I urge you to purchase from locally owned stores whenever possible to encourage small business ownership.

Conversion Charts

All measurements in this book are US volume.

US common conversions

1 Tbsp	=	3 tsp
1 Fluid Ounce	=	2 Tbsp
1 Cup	=	8 Ounces
1 Pint	=	2 Cups
1 Quart	=	2 Pints
1 Gallon	=	4 Quarts

Please note that 1 tsp US = .83 tsp UK

US to Metric conversions

1/4 tsp	=	1.25 mL
1/2 tsp	=	2.5 mL
1 tsp	=	5 mL
1 Tbsp	=	15 mL
1 Fluid Ounce	=	30 mL
1/4 Cup	=	60 mL
1/3 Cup	=	78 mL
1/2 Cup	=	118.2 mL
1 Cup	=	236.5 mL
1 Pint (U.S.)	=	473 mL
1 Quart (U.S.)	=	946 mL
1/2 inch	=	1.27 cm
2 inches	=	5.08 cm
3 inches	=	7.62 cm
15 inches	=	38.1 cm

Fahrenheit to Celsius conversions

300 F	=	148.89 C
325 F	=	162.78 C
350 F	=	176.67 C
375 F	=	190.56 C
400 F	=	204.44 C
425 F	=	218.33 C
450 F	=	232.22 C
500 F	=	260.00 C

Yeast conversions

1 packet (2-1/4 tsp.) active dry is the equivalent to:

1 cube fresh

1 packet quick rise

3/4 packet instant

Egg conversions

1 large egg (US) is approximately 2 oz. or 57 g which is equivalent to:

1 large egg (CA)

1 medium egg (EU)

1 large egg (AU)

1 standard "6" egg (NZ)

Tools & Tips

This book is going to teach you to work with normal household kitchen items to make great bread. Normal = nothing commercial, nothing intimidating, nothing fancy.

Thermometer:

There is one tool that is absolutely required for my recipes: a thermometer. Either traditional or digital style is fine. A few degrees in internal temperature is the difference between failure and success with bread, and check the calibration from time to time.

Calibration: place the end of the thermometer in a pot of boiling water. The water should be at a steady boil, and the tip of the thermometer should NOT touch the bottom of the pan. Wait for a minute, then check the reading. It should show 212 F / 100 C. If your thermometer shows a different number, then you can still use the thermometer, as long as you make sure you take this difference into account and adjust the recipe temperatures by the number of calibrated degrees over or under.

Pans:

If you do not have bread pans, then you can shape your breads and simply bake these on a half-sheet pan (aka cookie sheet or jelly roll pan). For your half-sheet pan, what you are looking for is a heavy sheet. You do not want an air-cushion built in or any other fancy features. Non-stick is okay, but not necessary. For baking pans, your personal choice of ceramic, silicone, metal, or glass is fine. For one recipe, I will note that you can use the ceramic liner of a crock-pot / slow-cooker, but ensure that yours is oven safe before use.

Bench Scraper:

Also known as a dough scraper, a bench scraper is useful for clearing off your work surface and for cutting a piece of dough into multiple pieces for rolls or individual loaves.

Pastry Brush:

Purchase an actual pastry brush, not a paint brush. Make sure that it is only used for baking work. Either natural or silicone bristles are fine. Do not use any brush that has touched paint, and do not use a brush that has been used with seafood and fish, no matter how well it has been washed, just do not use it. Please.

Parchment Paper:

Although not necessary, this useful tool will save you cleaning time. Plus, it will help protect the bottoms of your loaves from browning too fast.

Spritzer Bottle:

Keep an oil mister (spritzer) or spray bottle of non-stick cooking vegetable oil on hand at all times. I have a refillable oil mister pump bottle to save money compared to pre-loaded spray bottles and to save both the environment and my health from the propellants used for aerosol sprays.

Olive Oil:

When to use which kind? Basic **Olive Oil** is used any time you are going to apply heat to it with cooking or baking. **Extra Virgin Olive Oil** is used any time that it is not going to be heated, such as when mixed with herbs or balsamic vinegar for dipping bread or when in a salad dressing recipe.

Tips:

Makin adjustments in your baking is normal, depending upon your altitude as well the temperature and humidity, which changes throughout the year. Note changes with your recipes as well as the conditions/seasons that inspired these.

Baking times are approximations, not laws. The slightest changes in recipes and individual oven calibrations will change baking times each time you bake breads. If your bread looks "done" 15 minutes early, then check the internal temperature with your thermometer. Temperature "done" is more critical for awesome bread than time "done".

When there are multiple tools or methods that are equivalent, I show you with "A / B" writing in the recipe.

Kneading

Lightly shake 1-2 Tbsp. flour (same flour as used in the recipe) onto clean countertop in approximately a 12 inch square area to cover lightly the kneading work surface (called dusting with flour).

Scrape dough out of bowl with spatula into middle of floured area.

Step 1:
Hold your arms outstretched, hands palm up, fingers together, and fingertips touching, then using the "littlest finger" edge of the hand, scoop under edge of dough farthest away from you, getting a few inches underneath.

Step 2:
Gently and with a smooth motion fold that edge toward you and on top of itself until the edges are close to meeting, then release the edge.

Step 3:
Turn both wrists so that your fingers point away from you, then place the palms of your hands on top of the dough with your wrists at the edge closest to you.

Step 4:
In a combined movement, push dough using only the palms in a forward and slightly downward motion until your arms reach full extension.

Step 5:
Move hands to sides of the dough, rotate hands palm up, with fingers still together, and using fingertips, gently lift edges just enough to rotate the entire dough piece a "1/4 turn" clockwise, noting that you do not have to pick up the entire piece off of the surface.

Step 6: Repeat Step 1 to Step 5, for the recipe's listed time, to reach desired consistency as listed in the recipe.

Helpful Kneading Hints:
Hint 1:
If dough is sticking to your hands/fingers at any point in the kneading process, then first flip the dough over a few times in the flour on the work surface until the sticky parts are covered. Second, if you need more flour than that, then having an extra cup of flour (same as used in the recipe) nearby will allow you to add a little flour at a time to dust overtop the dough until the sticky parts are covered.

Hint 2:
If you get sticky dough on your hands, then remove it by adding a little flour to your hands and rubbing it around in the same motions as washing your hands, until the dough falls off.

Hint 3:
As you push forward and down, this process should not tear the skin of the dough. The "skin" will get stronger as your kneading process repeats, but continue to be gentle throughout the repeating steps.

Hint 4:

There are two main errors possible with kneading: too much and too little. Of the two, the error of too little is better to do. Since most of these recipes use bread flour, the bread dough will develop gluten strands quickly, so a few minutes of kneading will produce enough structural strands to support most breads. Over-kneading can result in too-tough bread.

Hint 5:

I recommend that you make notes in this book about the results and the time spent kneading each recipe so that you can fine tune your recipes to meet your style. Remember, no two people knead bread exactly the same way or at the same pace. You will become quicker as you gain confidence, but correct technique is more important than speed.

Hint 6:

When kneading, be gentle. The dough did not steal your car, so do not make it suffer. Also, you should not be suffering from a few minutes of kneading. Remember that we are just helping it develop gluten, and that this can be a relaxing process with my specific, simplified steps and maybe some groovy background music.

Hint 7:

Some kneading recipes will give the alternate of using an electric mixer with a dough hook. Beware: using a dough hook will wear out your mixer faster. Also, if the recipe does not mention a mixer option, then please do not use it and just do the kneading by hand, as that is important for some breads to work correctly.

Common Problems

Oops, I forgot that I needed ____ :

It is best if you set up your ingredients as if you are doing a cooking show on television - measure out everything before you start. This way you ensure you have enough of everything, that eggs are good, etc.

Dough is too wet:

It is okay if your dough is still wet after following directions, as you can just add a little more flour. Keep adding very small amounts flour at a time, mixing well after each small addition, until the dough becomes workable. If kneading, then do not push hard, as you do not want to tear the dough.

Dough is not rising:

First, make sure that your yeast is alive. When you added the warm water and flour, you should have seen bubbles appear, as the yeast begins to feed. Second, if your yeast is good, then the dough may simply need more time. The times for rising listed in the book are not exact rules. For example, if the weather is warm and moist, then you may find your dough rising in half the time. Adjust rise timing to what you are seeing, even if the rise time is different than I suggested.

Time is up, but bread is not browning:

Patience is needed, as the baking and browning times are approximations. It is worth waiting extra minutes for the bread to finish to complete awesomeness.

Recipes

Anadama Bread

Anise Bread with Orange Glaze

Bagels

Baguettes

Banana Bread

Bannock / "Indian Fry Bread"

Biscuits

Brotchen

Buttermilk Bread

Buttermilk, Apple, & Cinnamon Bread

Buttermilk & Blueberry Bread

Buttermilk & Cranberry Bread

Challah

Chocolate Bread

Ciabatta

Cinnamon Rolls

Cinnamon & Raisin Swirl Bread

Cornbread

Dampfnudeln

Dinner Rolls

Greek Village Bread

Hands-Off Bread

Honey Bread

Naan

Oat Bread

Pizza Dough

Pretzel Rolls / Buns

Pullman Loaf: Wheat

Pullman Loaf: White

Pullman Loaf: Rye

Pumpkin Bread

Rosemary Rolls

Sausage Bread

Scones: Basic

Scones: Apple Awesomeness

Scones: Blueberry & Orange

Scones: Lemon & Candied Ginger

Scones: Raspberry & White Chocolate

Shortbread

Soda Bread

Tortillas

Bonus Recipes

Anadama Bread

"ah nah dah mah"

There are numerous tales about the origins of Anadama bread. I will tell you the one that I heard when I was introduced to this hearty bread: Anadama originated in the New England states region. After being out to sea for good bit of time, a married fisherman came home on one cold, rainy evening to find out that his wife, Anna, had left him during his last fishing trip. She had taken almost everything with her. She left him without furniture, clothing, or anything in the pantry except for a little cornmeal, molasses, and flour. As he worked to put these few ingredients together to make something for his supper, he yelled, "Anna! Damn Her!" The result of his work that night was this delicious bread, and so it was named. However, New Englanders wanted to make the name of the bread more family friendly, so they took to calling the bread "Anadama" instead. No matter which way you call it, you will find it delicious!

Ingredients:
1/2 cup cornmeal
1/2 cup water, room temperature
1/2 cup water (80 to 100 degrees)
2 & 1/4 cups bread flour
1 tsp active dry yeast
3/4 tsp salt
3 Tbsp black strap molasses
1 Tbsp butter, room temperature

Directions:
Step 1: (the evening before)
In a bowl, add cornmeal and water, mix with a spoon / spatula to combine well. Cover and allow to soak overnight on the countertop. **If you do not have time for this step the evening before**, then in a pot, on medium heat, add cornmeal and water, then bring to a boil, remove the pot from the heat, and set aside for 10 minutes.

Step 2:
In a bowl, add the pre-prepared cornmeal/water mixture, water, flour, and yeast, then stir with a spoon / spatula to combine well.

Step 3:
Add salt, molasses, and butter, then stir with a spoon / spatula to combine until the dough begins to come together as a large clump.

Step 4:
Knead for 3 to 5 minutes until smooth and pliable. **Or** put in an electric mixer with dough hook attachment and mix in the bowl for 3 to 5 minutes on medium speed, only adding a little extra flour if sticky.

Step 5:
Lightly coat **a 5 x 9 inch loaf / bread pan** with non-stick cooking oil spray. **Or** if you do not have a 5 x 9 pan, then use a half-sheet pan.

Step 6:
Transfer the dough into the loaf / bread pan and shape into a loaf form. Lightly coat top of the dough with non-stick cooking oil spray. Cover pan loosely with plastic wrap / film. Set aside 1 to 1 & 1/2 hours on countertop (dough will rise to top of pan and be doubled in volume when ready). **Or** shape dough into an elongated loaf and place on the half-sheet pan. Lightly coat dough with non-stick cooking oil spray. Do not cover. Set aside 1 to 1 & 1/2 hours on countertop (dough will be doubled in volume when ready).

Step 7:
Preheat oven to 350 degrees

Step 8:
Place the pan / sheet into the pre-heated oven, on the middle rack. Bake for 40 to 50 minutes, until golden-brown on top and middle of loaf registers 185 degrees on your thermometer.

Step 9:
Remove the bread from the loaf / bread pan by turning upside down, then place bread "right side up" directly on a wire rack to cool. **Or** remove the bread from the sheet pan with a spatula, then place bread directly on a wire rack to cool.

Step 10:
Wait 10 minutes, then cut and serve.

Fresh Storage:

Once cooled to room temperature, cover the bread with plastic film / wrap or place in a plastic sealable bag and store in the refrigerator. Do not reheat. Use within 1 week.

Frozen Storage:

Once cooled to room temperature, cover the bread with plastic wrap or place in a plastic sealable bag, move to refrigerator until completely cooled, then move to freezer. Remove from freezer and place on countertop to thaw before use. Do not reheat. May be frozen up to 1 month.

Your Notes:

_____

_____

Anise Bread with Orange Glaze

Ingredients:
1/2 cup warm milk (80 to 100 degrees)
2 & 1/4 tsp active dry yeast
1/3 cup sugar
1/3 cup orange juice, room temperature
1/3 cup butter, melted
1/2 tsp salt
2 Tbsp anise seeds
2 eggs, yolks only
3 cups flour
1 cup powdered sugar
2 Tbsp orange juice

Directions:
Step 1:
In a bowl, add warm milk, yeast, and sugar , then stir with a spoon / spatula to combine well. Set aside for 5 minutes.

Step 2:
Add orange juice, butter, salt, anise seeds, yolks, and flour, then stir with a spoon / spatula to combine well.

Step 3:
Knead 3 to 4 minutes, until smooth and pliable. **Or** put in an electric mixer with dough hook attachment and mix in the bowl for 3 to 4 minutes on medium speed, only adding a little extra flour if sticky.

Step 4:
Divide dough into 3 equal size pieces.

Step 5:
Take 1 piece of dough and roll into a 15 inch long, log-shaped piece of even thickness. You may roll this out with your hands on the floured countertop, **or** you may raise your hands above the countertop, with the piece hanging down and roll dough between your hands, flipping the dough and moving your hands to different holding places to roll into a uniform thickness. You may gently stretch the dough as you are rolling it, in order to achieve the desired length of 15 inches long.

Step 6:
Place the dough strand on a half-sheet pan lengthwise, leaving approximately 3 inches between dough pieces.

Step 7:
Repeat Step 6 to Step 7 until 3 strands are on the pan, with the **ends** "lined up" lengthwise evenly with each other.

Step 8:
Braid these 3 strands (much like you would a person's hair for Step 8-C to 8-F):

8-A   Turn the pan lengthwise so that the 3 strands are pointing toward you.

8-B   Keep in mind that the **ends** of the strands **farthest** away from you will need to **stay on the pan** while you are braiding in this direction.

8-C   From the ends closest to you, pick up the strand farthest to the left, at the bottom edge and **without moving the very top few inches of the strand**, move the rest of the strand to lay between the 2 strands still laying completely on the pan.

8-D   From the ends closest to you, pick up the strand that is now the farthest to the right, at the bottom edge and **without moving the very top few inches of the strand**, move the rest of the strand to lay between the 2 strands still laying completely on the pan.

8-E   Repeat Step 8-C to 8-D until you do not have enough length on the strands to braid anymore. The braided strands should be touching each other throughout the braid and with uniform "tension" so that the braid is uniform and the dough is in an overall straight line.

8-F   Turn the pan around 180 degrees so that you are looking at the braided strands from the opposite side.

8-G   Using your **left hand, pick up the strand farthest to the left** and lift it until you get to the part that is braided, then hold that there to wait. Using your **right hand, pick up the middle stand** and lift it until you get to the part that is braided. Make the strands "trade places" by first laying down the strand in your left hand first and into the "middle position", then by next laying down the strand in your right hand to the "left position". (You are braiding "in reverse" here by placing the side strands "under" instead of "over" as done in the first part.)

8-H   Using your **right hand, pick up the strand farthest to the right** and lift it until you get to the part that is braided, then hold that there to wait. Using your **left hand, pick up the middle stand** and lift it until you get to the part that is braided. Make the strands "trade places" by first laying down the strand in your right hand first and into the "middle position", then by next laying down the strand in your left hand to the "right position".

8-I   Repeat Step 8-G to 8-H until you do not have enough length on the strands to braid anymore.

8-J   Pick up the edges of the 3 strands at the same time. Pinch the edges of 3 dough strands together and gently lift up so that you can fold the combined edge under the braided part so that the braid cannot unravel.

8-K   Turn the pan around 180 degrees.

8-L   Repeat Step 8-J to the other set of strand ends.

Step 9:
Set pan aside 1 to 2 hours, until braided dough has doubled in volume.

Step 10:
Preheat oven to 375 degrees.

Step 11:
Place the pan into the pre-heated oven, on the middle rack. Bake for 30 to 35 minutes, until golden brown on top and middle of loaf registers 180 degrees on your thermometer.

Step 12:
Remove the braided loaf from the pan with a spatula (or 2) and place directly on a wire rack to cool for 5 minutes.

Step 13:
In a bowl, add powdered sugar and orange juice, then whisk to combine well, until glaze is smooth.

Step 14:
Using a pastry brush, generously spread the glaze over all of bread's visible surface. If you have glaze remaining, then serve it with the sliced bread for dipping or spreading.

Step 15:
Wait another 10 minutes, then slice and serve.

Fresh Storage:

Once cooled to room temperature, cover the bread with plastic film / wrap or place in a plastic sealable bag and store in the refrigerator. Do not reheat. Use within 1 week.

Frozen Storage:

Once cooled to room temperature, cover the bread with plastic wrap or place in a plastic sealable bag, move to refrigerator until completely cooled, then move to freezer. Remove from freezer and place on countertop to thaw before use. Do not reheat. May be frozen up to 1 month.

Your Notes:

_____

_____

Bagels

Ingredients:
2 & 1/2 cups bread flour (divided into 1 cup and
1 & 1/2 cups)
1/2 tsp active dry yeast
1 Tbsp sugar
1 tsp salt
1 cup warm water (80 to 100 degrees)
1/2 tsp desired topping (salt, poppy seeds, dried herbs,
sesame seeds, etc.
Or The Cinnamon Crumbly-Awesomeness topping

Variations:

Chocolate Bagels:
2 Tbsp cocoa powder
Add to Step 1, after water.

Brown Sugar & Cinnamon Bagels:
1 tsp ground cinnamon
1 Tbsp brown sugar
Add to Step 1, after water.

Cinnamon Crumbly-Awesomeness Topping:
**Can be used in conjunction with Plain, Chocolate,
or Brown Sugar & Cinnamon Bagels, but
awesomeness is experienced at peak level when
used on the Brown Sugar & Cinnamon Bagels.**
1 tsp ground cinnamon
2 Tbsp sugar
1 Tbsp butter, softened

In a bowl, add cinnamon, sugar, and butter
With bare hands, coat butter a little bit with dry
mixture, then begin breaking up butter with a motion
similar to snapping your fingers with your thumb
moving across all fingers, while you mix the butter
more with the dry mixture, until the incorporated
mixture gritty in appearance and texture. Set aside.
Step 18 & 3/4: Use a table knife to gently spread the
mixture to the tops of the bagels.

Directions:
Step 1:
In a bowl, add 1 cup of flour, yeast, sugar, and water, then
stir with a spoon / spatula to combine well. Set aside for 5
minutes.

Step 2:
Add remaining flour and 1 tsp salt, then stir with a spoon /
spatula to combine well.

Step 3:
Knead for 5 minutes, until smooth and pliable.

Step 4:
Cut dough into 6 pieces.

Step 5:
For each of the 6 pieces of dough, cup your hand over the
top of the dough, then roll it around in tight circles on the
countertop, to shape it into a smooth and round ball. Set
each aside until the 6 pieces have been made into balls.

Step 6:
Using your bare pointer finger, poke a hole through the **center** of 1 ball until your fingertip is on the countertop. Leaving your finger in the dough, invert your hand so that your finger is pointing upwards. Twirl your dough finger in small circles until a dough ring forms and the hole from your finger would hold a quarter (or euro) coin. Set aside on a clean countertop.

Step 7:
Repeat Step 6 until all 6 dough rings are on the countertop.

Step 8:
Lightly coat dough rings with non-stick cooking vegetable oil spray.

Step 9:
Lightly drape plastic wrap / film over dough rings. Wait 15 to 30 minutes until dough rings have doubled in volume.

Step 10:
Preheat oven to 400 degrees.

Step 11:
Lightly coat a half-sheet pan with non-stick cooking vegetable oil spray. Set aside.

Step 12:
In a pot, on high heat, add 8 cups of water, until it boils.

Step 13:
Reduce heat to medium, and maintain to simmer.

Step 14:
Transfer 1 dough ring onto a slotted spoon, gently place the ring into the simmering water, and allow it to slide off of the slotted spoon.

Step 15:
Repeat Step 14 until 2 or 3 rings are in the water together.

Step 16:
Simmer for 1 minute. Then using a slotted spoon, turn over the ring, and simmer for 1 more minute.

Step 17:
With a slotted spoon, transfer the bagels, one at a time, onto the half-sheet pan.

Step 18:
Repeat Step 14 to Step 17, until 6 bagels are on the half-sheet pan.

Step 19:
Place the pan into the pre-heated oven, on the middle rack. Bake for 15 minutes, until golden brown on top.

Step 20:
Remove the bagels from the pan with a spatula and place these directly on a wire rack to cool.

Step 21:
Wait 5 minutes, then serve.

Fresh Storage:
Once cooled to room temperature, place bagels in a plastic sealable bag and store in the refrigerator. May reheat in the oven on a half-sheet pan uncovered or in a microwave uncovered. Use within 1 week.

Frozen Storage:
Once cooled to room temperature, place bagels in a plastic sealable bag, move to refrigerator until completely cooled, then move to freezer. Remove from freezer and place on countertop to thaw before use. May reheat in the oven on a half-sheet pan uncovered or in a microwave uncovered. May be frozen up to 1 month.

Your Notes:

_____

_____

Baguettes

Ingredients:
4 & 1/2 cups bread flour
1 & 1/4 tsp active dry yeast
2 cups water, chilled
1 & 3/4 tsp salt
1 Tbsp cornmeal
1/2 cup boiling water

Directions:
Step 1:
In a bowl, add flour, yeast, and chilled water, then mix with a spoon / spatula until well combined.

Step 2:
Add salt, then mix with a spoon / spatula until well combined.

Step 3:
Cover bowl with plastic wrap / film and transfer to refrigerator for a minimum of 8 hours. Dough can be kept waiting for up to 3 days.

Step 4:
Transfer bowl from refrigerator to countertop and set aside for 2 hours.

Step 5:
Lightly dust a half-sheet pan with cornmeal. Set aside.

Step 6:
Knead 2 to 3 minutes. Do not use a mixer. Do not clean the flour from the countertop after kneading. If the flour was used up during kneading, then reapply flour dusting to the countertop.

Step 7:
Cut dough in half. Then, cut each half into half again, for a total of 4 pieces of dough.

Step 8:
Take 1 piece of dough and roll into a 16 inch long, log-shaped dough of even thickness. You may roll this out with your hands on the floured countertop, **or** you may raise your hands above the countertop, with the piece hanging down and roll dough between your hands, flipping the dough and moving your hands to different holding places to roll into a uniform thickness. You may gently stretch the dough as you are rolling it, in order to achieve the desired length of 16 inches long.

Step 9:
As you finish rolling each piece, place it on the half-sheet pan so that all 4 will fit lengthwise with uniform space between each one.

Step 10:
Repeat Step 7 to Step 8 until 4 dough pieces are on the pan.

Step 11:
Loosely cover the pan with plastic wrap / film. Allow baguette dough pieces to rise for 1 to 2 hours, until doubled in volume.

Step 12:
Place an oven rack on the lowest position. On that rack, place a cast-iron skillet or similar oven-safe item capable of retaining large amounts of heat for a long period of time. Place the other oven rack to the middle position with nothing on it. Preheat oven to 500 degrees.

Step 13:
Place the pan into the pre-heated oven, on the middle rack. Have your 1/2 cup of boiling water ready to use.
Attention! Keep in mind that you will need to do the next move quickly but **safely**, so protect yourself from a **possible steam burn** by holding your face and body as far away from the oven door area as possible, wearing oven mitts and a long-sleeved shirt, and with any additional safety measure you can do. Also, please have anyone watching you maintain a safe distance from the oven, especially children.
Then, holding the oven door handle with one hand and the 1/2 cup of boiling water in the other, quickly and carefully pour the water into the cast-iron skillet on the bottom rack, then quickly close the oven door. Immediately lower the temperature to 475 degrees and bake for 12 to 20 minutes, until golden-brown on top and middle of loaves register 205 degrees on your thermometer.

(This steaming process will give your bread that wonderful crisp exterior that you find in a great baguette without using a commercial steam-injection oven!)

Step 14:
Remove the baguettes from the sheet with a spatula and place these directly on a wire rack to cool.

Step 15:
Wait 5 minutes, then cut and serve.

Fresh Storage:
Once cooled to room temperature, cover the baguettes with plastic film / wrap or place in a plastic sealable bag and store in the refrigerator. May reheat in the oven on a half-sheet pan uncovered. Use within 1 week.

Frozen Storage:
Once cooled to room temperature, cover the baguettes with plastic wrap or place in a plastic sealable bag, move to refrigerator until completely cooled, then move to freezer. Remove from freezer and place on countertop to thaw before use. May reheat in the oven on a half-sheet pan uncovered. May be frozen up to 1 month.

Your Notes:

_____

_____

Banana Bread

Ingredients:
1 & 3/4 cups all-purpose flour
1 & 1/2 cups sugar
1/2 tsp baking soda
1/2 tsp baking powder
1/2 tsp ground cinnamon
1/2 tsp salt
2 eggs, whisked
1/2 cup butter, melted and cooled
1/4 cup milk
1 tsp vanilla extract
1 cup bananas, peeled then mashed and packed in the cup
    (ripe or over-ripe)

Variations:
1 cup walnuts, chopped
Add in Step 6 & 3/4

Directions:
Step 1:
Preheat oven to 325 degrees.

Step 2:
Lightly coat inside of 5 x 9 with non-stick cooking vegetable oil spray. Set aside.

Step 3:
In a bowl, add bread flour, sugar, baking soda, baking powder, cinnamon, and salt, then whisk to combine well. Set aside.

Step 4:
In another bowl, add eggs, butter, milk and vanilla, then whisk to combine well.

Step 5:
Add banana, then using a whisk, re-mash and separate the packed banana until it is broken into many tiny pieces. Then, whisk the mix vigorously to distribute the banana bits evenly.

Step 6:
Add the dry ingredients mixture, then gently stir the mix with a spoon / spatula, several times to combine. Make sure that the dry and wet ingredients are fully combined by scraping the bottom of the mixing bowl several times to make sure there are no pockets of flour. The dough may look soupy.

Step 6 & 3/4:
Optional: Add nuts, then gently stir with a spoon / spatula a few times.

Step 7:
Transfer dough to 5 x 9 inch pan by pouring the mixture, then scraping the sides of the bowl with a spoon / spatula.

Step 8:
Smooth top of dough with spoon / spatula.

Step 9:
Place the pan into the pre-heated oven, on the middle rack. Bake for 80 minutes, until middle of loaf registers 180 degrees on your thermometer.

Step 10:
Remove pan from the oven and hold upside down over countertop to remove the bread from the pan. **Or** if the bread sticks to the pan, then stick a table-knife straight down between the edge of the pan and the bread, then "run" the knife along all the edges to trace the outline of the bread away from the pan, then hold the pan upside down again to remove the bread from the pan.

Step 11:
Transfer bread onto a wire rack, "right side" side up.

Step 12:
Wait 10 minutes, then slice and serve.

Fresh Storage:
Once cooled to room temperature, cover bread with plastic film / wrap or place in a plastic sealable bag and store in the refrigerator. Use within 1 week. Do not reheat.

Frozen Storage:
Once cooled to room temperature, cover bread with plastic wrap or place in a plastic sealable bag, move to refrigerator until completely cooled, then move to freezer. Remove from freezer and place on countertop to thaw before use. May be frozen up to 1 month. Do not reheat.

Your Notes:

_____

_____

Bannock / "Indian Fry Bread"

Ingredients:
4 cups all-purpose flour
3 Tbsp sugar
4 tsp baking powder
1 tsp salt
1 & 2/3 cup water (80 to 100 degrees)
1/3 cup powdered milk
1/3 cup vegetable oil
2 cups solid vegetable shortening / "Crisco"

Special Note:
This bread is special to me. I grew up eating fry bread at home and at Pow-Wows, where we danced as children.

It is food that came from hardship. The origins of fry bread can be found in the government rations that were delivered to reservations for Native tribes. Very spartan, these rations consisted of very few items that would constitute a meal, and Natives had to be creative with what they had.

This is my mother's recipe. Enjoy!

Directions:
Step 1:
In a bowl, add flour, sugar, baking powder, salt, water, powdered milk, and oil, then mix with a spoon / spatula to combine well.

Step 2:
Knead 3 to 5 minutes, until smooth. Do not use a mixer.

Step 3:
Break into pieces roughly the size of a deck of cards.

Step 4:
In a cast-iron frying pan (cast iron is best, but another high edged pot or pan will do), on medium heat, bring shortening to about 350 degrees. Adjust heat level to maintain 350 degrees.

Step 5:
Set up a dinner-size plate covered with several paper-towels laying on top to use. **Or** use a plate covered with a folded brown-paper-bag. Set aside.

Step 6:
Stretch, by hand, 1 piece into an 8 inch circle.

Step 7:
Gently lower 1 circle of dough into the frying pan, by holding 1 edge and gently laying it down flat. Fry for 1 to 2 minutes, until golden-brown. Use tongs to grasp 1 edge and to flip the circle of dough over. Fry for another 1 to 2 minutes, until golden brown.

Step 8:
Using tongs, grasp 1 edge and transfer fry bread to paper / bag covered plate set up from Step 5 so that the fry bread lays down flat.

Step 9:

If you want to make fry bread as a dessert, then immediately sprinkle it on both sides with either confection, powdered, or granulated white sugar. Then, using tongs, grasp 1 edge and transfer the fry bread to plain serving platter.

Or if you want to have fry bread with your meal as bread or to make into tacos, then leave the fry bread for 1 minute on the plate. Then, using tongs, grasp 1 edge, hold the fry bread above the drain plate to allow oil in "pockets" to drain for a few seconds, and then stack on a plain serving platter.

Step 10: Repeat Step 5 to Step 9 for each remaining piece of dough, until all dough has been fried. Continue to place new paper towels or bags on the drain plate as needed. Continue to stack finished fry bread on a plain serving platter.

Serving Suggestion:

For tacos, serve fry bread with salsa, ground venison cooked with onions, taco seasoning, diced tomatoes, shredded lettuce, shredded cheddar cheese, and sour cream. Incredible!

Fresh Storage:

Once cooled to room temperature, cover the fry bread with plastic film / wrap or place in a plastic sealable bag and store in the refrigerator. May not reheat. Use within 1 week.

Frozen Storage:

Do not freeze.

Your Notes:

_____

_____

Biscuits

Ingredients:
2 cups all-purpose flour
1 Tbsp baking powder
1 Tbsp sugar
1 tsp salt
1/4 cup shortening (solid)
2 Tbsp butter, cold out of refrigerator
2/3 cup milk
1-2 Tbsp all-purpose flour for shaking onto work surface
1/4 cup all-purpose flour in a bowl for using cutter tool

Variations:
Garlic Cheese Biscuits:
1 tsp garlic powder
Add to Step 2, before mixing.
2/3 cup of grated cheddar cheese
Add to Step 3, just after the butter is added.

Herb Biscuits:
1 tsp garlic powder
Add to Step 2, before mixing.
1 tsp of one dried herb of your choice (rosemary,
    thyme, chive, etc
Add to Step 2 before mixing.

Directions:
Step 1:
Preheat oven to 450 degrees.

Step 2:
In a bowl, add flour, baking powder, sugar, and salt, then mix with a spoon / spatula to combine.

Step 3:
Add shortening and butter. With bare hands, coat shortening and butter a little bit with dry mixture, then begin breaking up shortening and butter with a motion similar to snapping your fingers with your thumb moving across all fingers, while you mix the shortening and butter more with the dry mixture, until the dough is mealy and gritty in appearance and texture (no pieces bigger than pea-sized).

Step 4:
Add milk, then stir with spoon / spatula to combine well.

Step 5:
Knead 10 times. Do not use a mixer.

Step 6:
Using a rolling pin, roll out the dough until it is about 1/2 inch thick all over.

Step 7:
Using a round "cookie" cutter or "biscuit" cutter or the rim of a drinking glass (2 or 3 inches across), dip cutter into bowl of flour, push cutter straight down into dough - do not twist - pull the cutter straight up, place cut piece onto a half-sheet pan. (Repeat Step 7 until all biscuits have been cut out and arranged onto the pan having left 2 inches between biscuits.)

Step 8:
Place the sheet into the pre-heated oven, on the middle rack. Bake for 10 to 15 minutes, until golden-brown on top.

Step 9:
Remove the biscuits from the sheet with a spatula and place these directly on a wire rack to cool.

Step 10:
Wait 5 minutes and serve.

Fresh Storage:
Once cooled to room temperature, place biscuits in a plastic sealable bag and store in the refrigerator. May reheat in the oven on a half-sheet pan uncovered or in a microwave uncovered. Use within 1 week.

Frozen Storage:
Once cooled to room temperature, place biscuits in a plastic sealable bag, move to refrigerator until completely cooled, then move to freezer. Remove from freezer and place on countertop to thaw before use. May reheat in the oven on a half-sheet pan uncovered or in a microwave uncovered. May be frozen up to 1 month.

Your Notes:

_____

_____

Brotchen (German Roll)

Ingredients:
1 cup warm water (80 to 100 degrees)
2 tsp active dry yeast
3 cups all-purpose flour (divided into 1 cup and 2 cups)
1 tsp sugar
1 tsp salt
1 egg, "white" only
1 tsp water

Directions:
Step 1:
Lightly coat a half-sheet pan with non-stick cooking vegetable oil spray. Set aside.

Step 2:
In a bowl, add warm water, yeast, and 1 cup flour, then mix with spoon / spatula to combine well. Set aside for 5 minutes.

Step 3:
Add remaining flour, sugar, and salt, then mix with spoon / spatula to combine well.

Step 4:
Knead for 3 to 4 minutes until smooth and pliable. **Or** put in an electric mixer with dough hook attachment and mix in the bowl for 3 to 4 minutes on medium speed, only adding a little extra flour if sticky.

Step 5:
Do not clean the flour from the countertop after kneading. If the flour was used up during kneading, then reapply flour dusting to the countertop.

Step 6:
With a scraper or table knife, cut dough into 6 equal pieces.

Step 7:
For each of the 6 pieces of dough, cup your hand over the top of the dough, then roll it around in tight circles on the countertop, to shape it into a smooth and round ball.

Step 8:
As you finish rolling each dough piece into a ball, place it on the half-sheet pan so that all 6 will fit with uniform space between each.

Step 9:
When all 6 dough balls are on the half-sheet, lightly coat the tops of the balls with non-stick cooking vegetable oil spray. Set aside. Allow dough balls to rise for 1/2 to 1 hour, until doubled in volume.

Step 10:
Preheat oven to 450 degrees.

Step 11:
In a bowl, add egg white and 1 tsp water, then whisk, until frothy.

Step 12:
With a pastry brush, gently and lightly coat each roll with egg white mixture, covering all visible surfaces.

Step 13:
Place the pan into the pre-heated oven, on the middle rack. Bake for 15 to 20 minutes, until golden-brown on top and middle of rolls register 180 degrees on your thermometer.

Step 14:
Remove the rolls from the sheet with a spatula and place these directly on a wire rack to cool.

Step 15:
Wait 5 minutes, then serve.

Fresh Storage:
Once cooled to room temperature, place rolls in a plastic sealable bag and store in the refrigerator. May reheat in the oven on a half-sheet pan uncovered or in a microwave uncovered. Use within 1 week.

Frozen Storage:
Once cooled to room temperature, place rolls in a plastic sealable bag, move to refrigerator until completely cooled, then move to freezer. Remove from freezer and place on countertop to thaw before use. May reheat in the oven on a half-sheet pan uncovered or in a microwave uncovered. May be frozen up to 1 month.

Your Notes:

_____

_____

Buttermilk Bread

Ingredients:
2 cups all-purpose flour
1/2 cup sugar
1 & 1/2 tsp baking powder
1/2 tsp baking soda
1 tsp salt
1 cup buttermilk
1 egg, whisked
1/4 cup butter, melted

Directions:
Step 1:
Preheat oven to 350 degrees.

Step 2:
Lightly coat a 5 by 9 inch loaf / bread pan with non-stick cooking vegetable oil spray.

Step 3:
In a bowl, add the flour, sugar, baking powder, baking soda, and salt, then whisk to combine well. Set aside.

Step 4:
In another bowl, add buttermilk, egg, and butter, then whisk to combine well.

Step 5:
Add dry mixture, then stir with a spoon / spatula to combine well. Make sure that the dry and wet ingredients are fully combined by scraping the bottom of the mixing bowl several times to make sure there are no pockets of flour. The dough may look soupy.

Step 6:
Transfer dough to 5 x 9 inch pan by pouring the mixture, then scraping the sides of the bowl with a spoon / spatula.

Step 7:
Smooth top of dough with spoon / spatula.

Step 8:
Place the pan into the pre-heated oven, on the middle rack. Bake for 50 to 60 minutes, until golden-brown on top and middle of loaf registers 180 degrees on your thermometer.

Step 9:
Remove pan from the oven and place on a wire rack to cool for 15 minutes.

Step 10:
Hold upside down over countertop to remove the bread from the pan. **Or** if the bread sticks to the pan, then stick a table-knife straight down between the edge of the pan and the bread, then "run" the knife along all the edges to trace the outline of the bread away from the pan, then hold the pan upside down again to remove the bread from the pan.

Step 11:
Transfer bread onto a wire rack, "right side" side up.

Step 12:
Wait 10 minutes, then slice and serve.

Fresh Storage:

Once cooled to room temperature, cover bread with plastic film / wrap or place in a plastic sealable bag and store in the refrigerator. Use within 1 week. Do not reheat.

Frozen Storage:

Once cooled to room temperature, cover bread with plastic wrap or place in a plastic sealable bag, move to refrigerator until completely cooled, then move to freezer. Remove from freezer and place on countertop to thaw before use. May be frozen up to 1 month. Do not reheat.

Your Notes:

_____

_____

Buttermilk, Apple, & Cinnamon Bread

Ingredients:
2 cups all-purpose flour
1/2 cup sugar
1 & 1/2 tsp baking powder
1/2 tsp baking soda
1 tsp salt
1 tsp ground cinnamon
1 cup buttermilk
1 egg, whisked
1 tsp vanilla
1/4 cup butter, melted
1 cup apples, peeled and cored, then cut into 1/4" pieces

Directions:
Step 1:
Preheat oven to 350 degrees.

Step 2:
Lightly coat a 5 by 9 inch loaf / bread pan with non-stick cooking vegetable oil spray.

Step 3:
In a bowl, add the flour, sugar, baking powder, baking soda, salt, and cinnamon, then whisk to combine well. Set aside.

Step 4:
In another bowl, add buttermilk, egg, vanilla, and butter, then whisk to combine well.

Step 5:
Add dry mixture, then stir with a spoon / spatula to combine well. Make sure that the dry and wet ingredients are fully combined by scraping the bottom of the mixing bowl several times to make sure there are no pockets of flour. The dough may look soupy.

Step 6:
Add apple pieces, then use a spatula to stir gently.

Step 7:
Transfer dough to 5 x 9 inch pan by pouring the mixture, then scraping the sides of the bowl with a spoon / spatula.

Step 8:
Smooth top of dough with spoon / spatula.

Step 9:
Place the pan into the pre-heated oven, on the middle rack. Bake for 50 to 60 minutes, until golden-brown on top and middle of loaf registers 180 degrees on your thermometer.

Step 10:
Remove pan from the oven and place on a wire rack to cool for 15 minutes.

Step 11:
Hold upside down over countertop to remove the bread from the pan. **Or** if the bread sticks to the pan, then stick a table-knife straight down between the edge of the pan and the bread, then "run" the knife along all the edges to trace the outline of the bread away from the pan, then hold the pan upside down again to remove the bread from the pan.

Step 12:
Transfer bread onto a wire rack, "right side" side up.

Step 13:
Wait 10 minutes, then slice and serve.

Fresh Storage:
Once cooled to room temperature, cover bread with plastic film / wrap or place in a plastic sealable bag and store in the refrigerator. Use within 1 week. Do not reheat.

Frozen Storage:
Once cooled to room temperature, cover bread with plastic wrap or place in a plastic sealable bag, move to refrigerator until completely cooled, then move to freezer. Remove from freezer and place on countertop to thaw before use. May be frozen up to 1 month. Do not reheat.

Your Notes:

_____

_____

Buttermilk & Blueberry Bread

Ingredients:
2 cups all-purpose flour
1/2 cup sugar
1 & 1/2 tsp baking powder
1/2 tsp baking soda
1 tsp salt
zest 1 lemon
1 cup buttermilk
1 egg, whisked
1 tsp vanilla
1/4 cup butter, melted
1 cup fresh or frozen blueberries

Directions:
Step 1:
Preheat oven to 350 degrees.

Step 2:
Lightly coat a 5 by 9 inch loaf / bread pan with non-stick cooking vegetable oil spray.

Step 3:
In a bowl, add the flour, sugar, baking powder, baking soda, salt, and zest, then whisk to combine well. Set aside.

Step 4:
In another bowl, add buttermilk, egg, vanilla, and butter, then whisk to combine well.

Step 5:
Add dry mixture, then stir with a spoon / spatula to combine well. Make sure that the dry and wet ingredients are fully combined by scraping the bottom of the mixing bowl several times to make sure there are no pockets of flour. The dough may look soupy.

Step 6:
Add blueberries, then use a spatula to stir gently to avoid staining the dough.

Step 7:
Transfer dough to 5 x 9 inch pan by pouring the mixture, then scraping the sides of the bowl with a spoon / spatula.

Step 8:
Smooth top of dough with spoon / spatula.

Step 9:
Place the pan into the pre-heated oven, on the middle rack. Bake for 50 to 60 minutes, until golden-brown on top and middle of loaf registers 180 degrees on your thermometer.

Step 10:
Remove pan from the oven and place on a wire rack to cool for 15 minutes.

Step 11:
Hold upside down over countertop to remove the bread from the pan. **Or** if the bread sticks to the pan, then stick a table-knife straight down between the edge of the pan and the bread, then "run" the knife along all the edges to trace the outline of the bread away from the pan, then hold the pan upside down again to remove the bread from the pan.

Step 12:
Transfer bread onto a wire rack, "right side" side up.

Step 13:
Wait 10 minutes, then slice and serve.

Fresh Storage:
Once cooled to room temperature, cover bread with plastic film / wrap or place in a plastic sealable bag and store in the refrigerator. Use within 1 week. Do not reheat.

Frozen Storage:
Once cooled to room temperature, cover bread with plastic wrap or place in a plastic sealable bag, move to refrigerator until completely cooled, then move to freezer. Remove from freezer and place on countertop to thaw before use. May be frozen up to 1 month. Do not reheat.

Your Notes:

_____

_____

Buttermilk & Cranberry Bread

Ingredients:
2 cups all-purpose flour
1/2 cup sugar
1 & 1/2 tsp baking powder
1/2 tsp baking soda
1 tsp salt
zest 1 orange
1 cup buttermilk
1 egg, whisked
1 tsp vanilla
1/4 cup butter, melted
1 cup dried cranberries

Directions:
Step 1:
Preheat oven to 350 degrees.

Step 2:
Lightly coat a 5 by 9 inch loaf / bread pan with non-stick cooking vegetable oil spray.

Step 3:
In a bowl, add the flour, sugar, baking powder, baking soda, salt, and zest, then whisk to combine well. Set aside.

Step 4:
In another bowl, add buttermilk, egg, vanilla, and butter, then whisk to combine well.

Step 5:
Add dry mixture, then stir with a spoon / spatula to combine well. Make sure that the dry and wet ingredients are fully combined by scraping the bottom of the mixing bowl several times to make sure there are no pockets of flour. The dough may look soupy.

Step 6:
Add cranberries, then use a spatula to stir gently to avoid staining the dough.

Step 7:
Transfer dough to 5 x 9 inch pan by pouring the mixture, then scraping the sides of the bowl with a spoon / spatula.

Step 8:
Smooth top of dough with spoon / spatula.

Step 9:
Place the pan into the pre-heated oven, on the middle rack. Bake for 50 to 60 minutes, until golden-brown on top and middle of loaf registers 180 degrees on your thermometer.

Step 10:
Remove pan from the oven and place on a wire rack to cool for 15 minutes.

Step 11:
Hold upside down over countertop to remove the bread from the pan. **Or** if the bread sticks to the pan, then stick a table-knife straight down between the edge of the pan and the bread, then "run" the knife along all the edges to trace the outline of the bread away from the pan, then hold the pan upside down again to remove the bread from the pan.

Step 12:
Transfer bread onto a wire rack, "right side" side up.

Step 13:
Wait 10 minutes, then slice and serve.

Fresh Storage:
Once cooled to room temperature, cover bread with plastic film / wrap or place in a plastic sealable bag and store in the refrigerator. Use within 1 week. Do not reheat.

Frozen Storage:
Once cooled to room temperature, cover bread with plastic wrap or place in a plastic sealable bag, move to refrigerator until completely cooled, then move to freezer. Remove from freezer and place on countertop to thaw before use. May be frozen up to 1 month. Do not reheat.

Your Notes:

_____

_____

Challah

Ingredients:
1 & 1/2 cup warm water (80 to 100 degrees)
2 tsp active dry yeast
1/4 cup honey
1/4 cup vegetable oil
3 eggs, whisked
1 & 1/2 tsp salt
4 cups all-purpose flour
1 egg, whisked
1 tsp water

Variations:
Raisin Challah:
1/2 cup raisins
Rinse raisins in hot tap water and set aside to dry, then add in Step 2, before stirring.

Challah Topping:
1 tsp poppy **Or** sesame seeds
Add Step 13 & 3/4, and sprinkle seeds on top of bread.

Directions:
Step 1:
In a bowl, add warm water, yeast, and honey, then stir with a spoon / spatula to combine well. Set aside for 5 minutes.

Step 2:
Add oil, salt, and flour, then stir with a spoon / spatula to combine well.

Step 3:
Add eggs, then stir with a spoon / spatula to combine well.

Step 4:
Knead 3 to 4 minutes, until smooth and pliable. **Or** put in an electric mixer with dough hook attachment and mix in the bowl for 3 to 4 minutes on medium speed, only adding a little extra flour if sticky.

Step 5:
Divide dough into 3 equal size pieces.

Step 6:
Take 1 piece of dough and roll into a 15 inch long, log-shaped piece of even thickness. You may roll this out with your hands on the floured countertop, **or** you may raise your hands above the countertop, with the piece hanging down and roll dough between your hands, flipping the dough and moving your hands to different holding places to roll into a uniform thickness. You may gently stretch the dough as you are rolling it, in order to achieve the desired length of 15 inches long.

Step 7:
Place the dough strand on a half-sheet pan lengthwise, leaving approximately 3 inches between dough pieces.

Step 8:
Repeat Step 6 to Step 7 until 3 strands are on the pan, with the **ends** "lined up" lengthwise evenly with each other.

Step 9:
Braid these 3 strands (much like you would a person's hair for Step 9-C to 9-F):

9-A   Turn the pan lengthwise so that the 3 strands are pointing toward you.

9-B   Keep in mind that the **ends** of the strands **farthest** away from you will need to **stay on the pan** while you are braiding in this direction.

9-C   From the ends closest to you, pick up the strand farthest to the left, at the bottom edge and **without moving the very top few inches of the strand**, move the rest of the strand to lay between the 2 strands still laying completely on the pan.

9-D   From the ends closest to you, pick up the strand that is now the farthest to the right, at the bottom edge and **without moving the very top few inches of the strand**, move the rest of the strand to lay between the 2 strands still laying completely on the pan.

9-E   Repeat Step 9-C to 9-D until you do not have enough length on the strands to braid anymore. The braided strands should be touching each other throughout the braid and with uniform "tension" so that the braid is uniform and the dough is in an overall straight line.

9-F   Turn the pan around 180 degrees so that you are looking at the braided strands from the opposite side.

9-G   Using your **left hand, pick up the strand farthest to the left** and lift it until you get to the part that is braided, then hold that there to wait. Using your **right hand, pick up the middle stand** and lift it until you get to the part that is braided. Make the strands "trade places" by first laying down the strand in your left hand first and into the "middle position", then by next laying down the strand in your right hand to the "left position". (You are braiding "in reverse" here by placing the side strands "under" instead of "over" as done in the first part.)

9-H   Using your **right hand, pick up the strand farthest to the right** and lift it until you get to the part that is braided, then hold that there to wait. Using your **left hand, pick up the middle stand** and lift it until you get to the part that is braided. Make the strands "trade places" by first laying down the strand in your right hand first and into the "middle position", then by next laying down the strand in your left hand to the "right position".

9-I   Repeat Step 9-G to 9-H until you do not have enough length on the strands to braid anymore.

9-J   Pick up the edges of the 3 strands at the same time. Pinch the edges of 3 dough strands together and gently lift up so that you can fold the combined edge under the braided part so that the braid cannot unravel.

9-K   Turn the pan around 180 degrees.

9-L   Repeat Step 9-J to the other set of strand ends.

Step 10:
Set pan aside 1 to 2 hours, until braided dough has doubled in volume.

Step 11:
Preheat oven to 375 degrees.

Step 12:
In a bowl, add 1 egg and 1 tsp water, then whisk until mixture is frothy.

Step 13:
Once the braided dough has doubled in volume, using a pastry brush, gently brush the bread with the frothy mixture. Use just enough of the mixture to lightly coat all the dough showing. Try to not brush or drip any mixture onto the pan. Remaining mixture should be transferred to the trash bin.

Step 13 & 3/4:
Optional: Apply topping to braided dough.

Step 14:
Place the pan into the pre-heated oven, on the middle rack. Bake for 30 to 35 minutes, until golden brown on top and middle of loaf registers 180 degrees on your thermometer.

Step 13:
Remove the braided loaf from the pan with a spatula (or 2 spatulas - 1 in each hand, if you have 2) and place directly on a wire rack to cool.

Step 14:
Wait 10 minutes, then serve.

Fresh Storage:

Once cooled to room temperature, cover the bread with plastic film / wrap or place in a plastic sealable bag and store in the refrigerator. Do not reheat. Use within 1 week.

Frozen Storage:

Once cooled to room temperature, cover the bread with plastic wrap or place in a plastic sealable bag, move to refrigerator until completely cooled, then move to freezer. Remove from freezer and place on countertop to thaw before use. Do not reheat. May be frozen up to 1 month.

Your Notes:

_____

_____

Chocolate Bread

Ingredients:
3/4 cup milk
1 cup bittersweet chocolate chips
4 Tbsp butter
6 Tbsp sugar
2 & 1/4 tsp active dry yeast
2 cups bread flour
3/4 tsp salt
1/2 tsp vanilla extract
1 egg, whisked

Variations:
Chocolate Nut Bread:
1/2 cup nuts, chopped (almonds, walnuts, or
                    hazelnuts)
Add in Step 5 & 3/4.

Directions:
Step 1:
In a pan, low heat, add milk, chocolate chips, and butter,
then stir frequently with a spoon / spatula, until chips are
melted but do not exceed 100 degrees on your thermometer.

Step 2:
In a bowl, add warm mixture, sugar, and yeast, then stir with
a spoon / spatula to combine well. Set aside for 5 minutes.

Step 3:
Lightly coat inside of 5 x 9 inch loaf / bread pan with non-
stick cooking vegetable oil spray. Set aside.

Step 4:
Add flour, salt, vanilla, and egg, then stir with a spoon /
spatula to combine well.

Step 5:
Knead for 5 minutes until smooth and pliable. **Or** put in an
electric mixer with dough hook attachment and mix in the
bowl for 5 minutes on medium speed, only adding a little
extra flour if sticky.

Step 5 & 3/4:
Optional: If adding nuts, then do so in the last minute of
kneading.

Step 6:
Using bare hands, shape dough to fit in a 5 x 9 inch pan,
smooth side up.

Step 7:
Transfer shaped dough to pan. Lightly coat bread with non-
stick cooking vegetable oil spray. Set aside 1 to 2 hours, until
loaf has doubled in size.

Step 8:
Preheat oven to 375 degrees.

Step 9:
Place the pan into the pre-heated oven, on the middle rack.
Bake for 50 to 60 minutes, until middle of loaf registers 180
degrees on your thermometer.

Step 10:
Remove pan from the oven and hold upside down over countertop to remove the bread from the pan. **Or** if the bread stick to the pan, then stick a table-knife straight down between the edge of the pan and the bread, then "run" the knife along all the edges to trace the outline of the bread away from the pan, then hold the pan upside down again to remove the bread from the pan.

Step 11:
Transfer bread onto a wire rack, "right side" side up.

Step 12:
Wait 15 minutes, then slice and serve.

Fresh Storage:
Once cooled to room temperature, cover the bread with plastic film / wrap or place in a plastic sealable bag and store on the countertop for up to 3 days **Or** store in the refrigerator and use within 1 week. Do not reheat.

Frozen Storage:
Once cooled to room temperature, cover the bread with plastic wrap or place in a plastic sealable bag, move to refrigerator until completely cooled, then move to freezer. Remove from freezer and place on countertop to thaw before use. May be frozen up to 1 month. Do not reheat.

Your Notes:

_____

_____

Ciabatta

Ingredients:
1 Tbsp cornmeal
3 & 3/4 cups all-purpose flour
1 & 1/2 cup warm water (80 to 100 degrees)
1 Tbsp olive oil
2 tsp active dry yeast
2 tsp salt
2 Tbsp olive oil
1/2 tsp all-purpose flour

Directions:
Step 1:
Lightly coat a half-sheet pan with cornmeal. Set aside.

Step 2:
In a bowl, add 3 & 3/4 cups flour, warm water, 1 Tbsp oil, and yeast, then stir with a spoon / spatula to combine well.

Step 3:
Add salt, then stir with a spoon / spatula to combine well. Set aside.

Step 4:
Use as much of the 2 Tbsp olive oil as you need to coat your bare hands generously. Any oil that is not needed should be spread onto dough.

Step 5:
Hold the dough over the bowl to allow oil to drip into the bowl and save your countertop from the mess! Use bare, oily hands to stretch the dough until it is twice the original size of the dough, then fold it in half.

Step 6:
Repeat Step 5 a total of 10 times.

Step 7:
Then, stretch dough until approximately 15 to 16 inches long and uniform in thickness and in an oblong shape.

Step 8:
Transfer dough to pan. Set aside 1 to 2 hours, until doubled in volume.

Step 9:
Preheat oven to 400 degrees.

Step 10:
When ready to bake, make sure that loaf does not exceed 5 inches in width. If it does, lightly coat your bare hands in a little olive oil, then using the palms of your hands, gently push the sides together until the dough is 5 inches in width.

Step 11:
Lightly sprinkle the top of the dough with 1/2 tsp flour.

Step 12:
Place the pan into the pre-heated oven, on the middle rack. Bake for 30 to 35 minutes, until golden brown on top and middle of loaf registers 190 degrees on your thermometer.

Step 13:
Remove the loaf from the pan with a spatula and place directly on a wire rack to cool.

Step 14:
Wait 10 minutes, then serve.

Fresh Storage:
Once cooled to room temperature, place bread in a plastic sealable bag and store in the refrigerator. May reheat in the oven on a half-sheet pan uncovered or in a microwave uncovered. Use within 1 week.

Frozen Storage:
Once cooled to room temperature, place bread in a plastic sealable bag, move to refrigerator until completely cooled, then move to freezer. Remove from freezer and place on countertop to thaw before use. May reheat in the oven on a half-sheet pan uncovered or in a microwave uncovered. May be frozen up to 1 month.

Your Notes:

_____

_____

Cinnamon Rolls

Ingredients:
3/4 cup brown sugar
1/4 cup sugar
2 tsp ground cinnamon
1/8 tsp ground cloves
1/8 tsp salt
1 cup milk
3 Tbsp butter
1/2 cup sugar
2 & 1/4 tsp active dry yeast
3 & 1/2 cups all-purpose flour (divided into 1 cup and
2 & 1/2 cups)

1 egg, whisked
1 tsp salt
1 Tbsp butter, melted
4 oz cream cheese, room temperature
1 cup powdered sugar
2 Tbsp heavy cream
1/2 tsp vanilla extract

Directions:
Step 1:
In a bowl, add brown sugar, granulated sugar, cinnamon, clove, and salt, then whisk to combine well. Set aside.

Step 2:
Lightly coat a 9 inch square baking pan with non-stick cooking vegetable oil spray.

Step 3:
In a pot, on medium-low heat, add milk and butter, then stir frequently with a spoon / spatula, until 80 to 90 degrees.

Step 4:
In a bowl, add warm mixture from pot, sugar, yeast, and 1 cup flour, then stir with a spoon / spatula to combine well. Set aside for 5 minutes.

Step 5:
Add egg, salt, and remaining flour, then stir with a spoon / spatula to combine well into dough.

Step 6:
Knead for 3 to 4 minutes until smooth and pliable. **Or** put in an electric mixer with dough hook attachment and mix in the bowl for 3 to 4 minutes on medium speed, only adding a little extra flour if sticky. Do not clean the flour from the countertop after kneading. If the flour was used up during kneading, then reapply flour dusting to the countertop.

Step 7:
With a rolling pin, roll dough into a 10 inch x 16 inch rectangle.

Step 8:
Using a pastry brush, spread melted butter evenly on the dough, except leaving a plain 1/2 inch border along the edges of the rectangle.

Step 9:
Transfer spice mixture from Step 1 onto rectangle. Spread mixture evenly, except leaving a plain 1/2 inch border along the edges of the rectangle.

Step 10:
With a 16 inch side closest to you, lift the edge and fold up and over an inch. Continue tightly rolling rectangle all the way across. Then, along the 16 inch edge, using bare hands, pinch the edge of the dough with the rolled dough to keep it from unrolling. This makes a "seam", as in sewing fabric.

Step 11:
Using a sharp knife (not serrated!), cut the rolled dough in half with a smooth, single cut (do not "saw" back and forth!). Then cut each half in half again, for 4 pieces. Then cut each quarter in half again, for 8 total rolls.

Step 12:
Transfer 8 rolls into the baking pan, placing a "cut side" up so that you can see the spice swirl. Make sure that there is uniform spacing around each roll.

Step 13:
Lightly coat "cut sides" of dough with non-stick cooking vegetable oil spray. Set aside for 30 to 45 minutes, until dough is doubled in volume and rolls are touching each other.

Step 14:
Preheat oven to 375 degrees.

Step 15:
Place the pan into the pre-heated oven, on the middle rack. Bake for 20 to 25 minutes, until golden brown on top and middle of rolls register 180 degrees on your thermometer.

Step 16:
In a bowl, add cream cheese, powdered sugar, cream, and vanilla, then whisk, until smooth. Set aside.

Step 17:
Remove pan from the oven and place on a wire rack to cool.

Step 18:
While rolls are cooling in the pan, using a spoon / spatula, spread cream cheese mixture evenly over the tops of the rolls, using all of the mixture.

Step 19:
Using a table knife, "run" the knife along all the edges to trace the outline of the 8 rolls.

Step 20:
Wait 10 minutes, then using a spatula, remove rolls 1 at a time to a serving dish, and serve warm.

Fresh Storage:

Once cooled to room temperature, cover rolls in pan with plastic film / wrap and store in the refrigerator. May reheat in the oven on a half-sheet pan or in the baking pan uncovered or in a microwave on a microwave-safe plate uncovered. Use within 1 week.

Frozen Storage:

Once cooled to room temperature, cover rolls in pan with plastic wrap and move to refrigerator until completely cooled, then move to freezer. Remove from freezer and place on countertop to thaw before use. May reheat in the oven on a half-sheet pan or in the baking pan uncovered or in a microwave on a microwave-safe plate uncovered. May be frozen up to 1 month.

Your Notes:

_____

_____

Cinnamon & Raisin Swirl Bread

Ingredients:
1 cup raisins
1/2 cup sugar
1 & 1/2 Tbsp ground cinnamon
1 egg, whisked
2 tsp warm water (80 to 100 degrees)
1 cup warm water (80 to 100 degrees)
1 Tbsp active dry yeast
1 cup milk
1/4 cup butter, melted
2 tsp salt
5 & 1/2 all-purpose flour

Directions:
Step 1:
In a bowl, add raisins and enough hot tap water to cover.
Soak for 10 minutes. Drain water out, then set aside.

Step 2:
Lightly coat 2 5 x 9 loaf / bread pans with non-stick
cooking vegetable oil spray. Set aside.

Step 3:
In a bowl, add sugar and cinnamon, then whisk to combine.
Set aside.

Step 4:
In a bowl, add egg and 2 tsp warm water, then whisk until
frothy. Set aside.

Step 5:
In a bowl, add warm water and yeast, then stir with a spoon / spatula to combine well. Set aside for 5 minutes.

Step 6:
Add milk, butter, and salt, , stir with a spoon / spatula to combine well.

Step 7:
Add flour, stir with a spoon / spatula to combine dough well.

Step 8:
Knead for 5 minutes until smooth and pliable. **Or** put in an electric mixer with dough hook attachment and mix in the bowl for 5 minutes on medium speed, only adding a little extra flour if sticky. During kneading / mixing, add in raisins gradually, until evenly dispersed. Do not clean the flour from the countertop after kneading. If the flour was used up during kneading, then reapply flour dusting to the countertop.

Step 9:
With a rolling pin, roll dough into a 10 inch x 16 inch rectangle.

Step 10:
Using a pastry brush, spread egg mixture from Step 3 evenly on the dough, except leaving a plain 1/2 inch border along the edges of the rectangle.

Step 11:
Transfer sugar mixture from Step 2 onto rectangle. Spread mixture evenly, except leaving a plain 1/2 inch border along the edges of the rectangle.

Step 12:
With a 16 inch side closest to you, lift the edge and fold up and over an inch. Continue tightly rolling rectangle all the way across. Then, along the 16 inch edge, using bare hands, pinch the edge of the dough with the rolled dough to keep it from unrolling. This makes a "seam", as in sewing fabric.

Step 13:
Using a sharp knife (not serrated!), cut the rolled dough in half with a smooth, single cut (do not "saw" back and forth!).

Step 14:
Transfer each dough half-roll into a 5 x 9 inch loaf / bread pan. Lightly coat the tops of the rolled doughs with non-stick cooking vegetable oil spray. Set aside for 60 to 90 minutes, until doughs have doubled in volume or reached the tops of the pans.

Step 15:
Preheat oven to 375 degrees.

Step 16:
Place the pans into the pre-heated oven, on the middle rack, side by side. Bake for 30 to 40 minutes, until middle of loaves register 180 degrees on your thermometer.

Step 17:
Remove pans from the oven and place on a wire cooling rack for 10 minutes.

Step 18:
Hold pans upside down over countertop to remove the breads from the pans. **Or** if the bread sticks to the pan, then stick a table-knife straight down between the edge of the pans and the breads, then "run" the knife along all the edges to trace the outline of the breads away from the pans, then hold the pans upside down again to remove the breads from the pans.

Step 19:
Transfer breads onto a wire rack, "right side" side up.

Step 20:
Wait 10 minutes, slice and serve warm.

Fresh Storage:
Once cooled to room temperature, cover breads with plastic film / wrap or place in a plastic sealable bag, and store in the refrigerator. Use within 1 week. Do not reheat.

Frozen Storage:
Once cooled to room temperature, cover breads with plastic wrap or place in a plastic sealable bag, and move to refrigerator until completely cooled, then move to freezer. Remove from freezer and place on countertop to thaw before use. May be frozen up to 1 month. Do not reheat.

Your Notes:

_____

_____

Cornbread

Ingredients:
1 cup cornmeal
1 cup all-purpose flour
1/2 tsp baking soda
1/2 tsp salt
1/2 cup butter, melted
1/3 cup sugar
2 eggs
1 cup buttermilk

Directions:
Step 1:
Preheat oven to 375 degrees.

Step 2:
Lightly coat an 8 x 8 inch pan with non-stick cooking oil spray.

Step 3:
In a bowl add cornmeal, flour, baking soda, and salt. Whisk well to combine these dry ingredients. Set aside.

Step 4:
In another bowl, add butter and sugar, then stir with a spoon until well combined. Allow to cool.

Step 5:
Add 1 egg, then stir vigorously with a fork until well combined.

Step 6:
Add 2nd egg, then stir vigorously with a fork until well combined.

Step 7:
To the bowl with butter, sugar, and eggs, add the entire bowl of dry ingredients, then add buttermilk on top.

Step 8:
At this point it is very important to not over-mix the dough, so... using a spatula, gently fold the mix over on top of itself five to seven times to combine the wet and dry ingredients, scraping the bottom of the bowl on each pass through the dough. Do **not** stir vigorously.

Step 9:
Gently pour mix into the oil-coated 8 x 8 inch pan, scraping sides of the bowl to get the entire mixture into the pan.

Step 10:
Place the pan into the pre-heated oven, on the middle rack. Bake for 30 to 35 minutes or until golden-brown on top. Check at the center of the bread with a toothpick inserted straight down and for approximately 3/4 the length of the toothpick. If done, then the toothpick should be "clean" or dry, without wet batter sticking to it.

Step 11:
Remove the pan and place it on a wire rack to cool.

Step 12:
Wait 5 minutes, then cut and serve.

Fresh Storage:

Once cooled to room temperature, cover the pan with plastic film / wrap and store in the refrigerator. May reheat in the oven covered with aluminum foil or in a microwave uncovered. Use within 1 week.

Frozen Storage:

Once cooled to room temperature, cover the pan with plastic wrap, move to refrigerator until completely cooled, then move to freezer. Remove from freezer and place on countertop to thaw before use. May reheat in the oven covered with aluminum foil or in a microwave uncovered. May be frozen up to 1 month.

Your Notes:

_____

_____

Dampfnudeln (German Rolls)

Ingredients:
1 cup warm water (80 to 100 degrees)
2 tsp active dry yeast
3 cups all-purpose flour
1 Tbsp sugar
1 tsp salt
1 Tbsp vegetable oil
1 egg, whisked
2 Tbsp solid vegetable shortening / "Crisco", divided into
      1 Tbsp & 1 Tbsp for 2 batches of cooking
1/2 cup warm water (80 to 100 degrees), divided into
      1/4 cup & 1/4 cup for 2 batches of cooking

Special Note:
This recipe was brought to the US by Lisa's Great Uncle Peter. In 1923, he and 6 family members immigrated by boat from Leimen, Germany, through Ellis Island in New York.

Uncle Peter first worked in the US in a German-style bakery, while he and the other family members learned English and became US citizens.

Uncle Peter joined the US military in 1941 and was stationed on a battle ship as a "gunner". Peter was very ill one fateful day and could not report to duty. During that day, the ship fell under attack, and every "gunner" on duty was killed. Peter was saddened by the loss of his friends, so he asked the man in charge of the ship's kitchen if he could bake something for "comfort food". The smell of Peter's baking drew the attention of an officer on the ship, and inquiry was made as to who was the baker. When Peter was identified, he was reassigned to the kitchen permanently, to bake and cook every day for the officers of the ship.

Peter was married to Coriel. Peter and Coriel had a bovine dairy business, a maple syrup business, and grew fruits, vegetables, and chickens at Maple Dell Farm in Ohio. A gaggle of mean-spirited geese was "security" for the farm, but we thought it was worth their trouble to visit Uncle Peter and Aunt Coriel, especially for meals, as his food was a comfort to us all. These rolls are so delicious that you will likely think it worth it to put up with mean geese to have these too! Guten Appetit!

Directions:

Step 1:
In a bowl, add water and yeast, then stir with a spoon / spatula to combine well. Set aside for 5 minutes.

Step 2:
Add remaining flour, sugar, salt, oil, and egg, then stir with a spoon / spatula to combine well.

Step 3:
Knead for 5 minutes, until smooth and pliable.

Step 4:
Cut dough into 6 pieces.

Step 5:
For each of the 6 pieces of dough, cup your hand over the top of the dough, then roll it around in tight circles on the countertop, to shape it into a smooth and round ball. Set each aside on the countertop, until the 6 pieces have been made into balls.

Step 6:
Lightly coat tops of balls with non-stick cooking vegetable oil spray. Wait 30 to 60 minutes until dough balls have doubled in volume.

Step 7:
In a pot with a lid / frying pan with a lid, on 1 dial setting less than medium heat, add 1 Tbsp shortening, then wait until it melts.

Step 8:
Transfer 1 dough ball onto a slotted spoon, gently place the ring into the melted shortening, and allow it to slide off of the slotted spoon.

Step 9:
Repeat Step 8 until 3 dough balls are in the pot / pan together.

Attention! Keep in mind that you will need to do the next move quickly but **safely**, so protect yourself from a **possible steam burn** by holding your face and body as far away from the pot / pan area as possible, wearing oven mitts and a long-sleeved shirt, and with any additional safety measure you can do. Also, please have anyone watching you maintain a safe distance from the oven, especially children.

Step 10:
Hold the lid in 1 hand and the 1/4 cup warm water in the other hand. Quickly pour the water into the pot / pan, then immediately and quickly put the lid on.

Step 11:
Cook for 6 minutes, without removing the lid to "peek"!

Step 12:
Remove lid and set aside. Then using a slotted spoon, turn over the dough rolls, and cook for 1 more minute, until golden-brown on top.

Step 13:
With a slotted spoon, transfer the rolls, one at a time, onto a serving plate.

Step 14:
Repeat Step 7 to Step 13, until all 6 rolls are on a serving plate.

Step 15:
Wait 5 minutes, then serve.

These Dampfnudeln rolls can be eaten as dinner rolls with a meal, or these can be sliced in half for excellent buns for sandwiches, including deli / sliced meats, veggie burgers, hamburgers, & bison burgers.

Fresh Storage:

Once cooled to room temperature, place rolls in a plastic sealable bag and store in the refrigerator. May reheat in the oven on a half-sheet pan uncovered or in a microwave uncovered. Use within 1 week.

Frozen Storage:

Once cooled to room temperature, place rolls in a plastic sealable bag, move to refrigerator until completely cooled, then move to freezer. Remove from freezer and place on countertop to thaw before use. May reheat in the oven on a half-sheet pan uncovered or in a microwave uncovered. May be frozen up to 1 month.

Your Notes:

_____

_____

Dinner Rolls

Ingredients:
1 cup milk
1/3 cup butter
2 & 1/4 tsp active dry yeast
4 cups all-purpose flour (separated into 1 cup and 3 cups)
1/3 cup sugar
1 tsp salt
2 eggs, whisked
1/4 cup butter, melted

Variations:
Herb Dinner Rolls:
1 Tbsp of your favorite choice of fresh, chopped herbs, **Or** 2 tsp of your favorite choice of dried herbs Add in Step 2, along with the sugar, salt, and eggs.

Directions:
Step 1:
Lightly coat a half-sheet pan with non-stick cooking vegetable oil spray. Set aside.

Step 2:
In a pot, add milk and butter, warm on medium-low heat until 80 to 100 degrees.

Step 3:
Transfer warmed mixture to a bowl. Add yeast and 1 cup flour, then mix with spoon / spatula to combine well. Set aside for 5 minutes.

Step 4:
Add remaining flour, then mix with spoon / spatula to combine well.

Step 5:
Add sugar, salt, and eggs, then mix with spoon / spatula to combine well.

Step 6:
Knead for 2 to 3 minutes until smooth and pliable. **Or** put in an electric mixer with dough hook attachment and mix in the bowl for 2 to 3 minutes on medium speed, only adding a little extra flour if sticky.

Step 7:
Cut dough in half. Then, cut each half into half again. Then, cut each quarter in half again. Then cut each eighth in half again, for a total of 16 pieces of dough. Do not clean the flour from the countertop after kneading. If the flour was used up during kneading, then reapply flour dusting to the countertop.

Step 8:
For each of the 16 pieces of dough, cup your hand over the top of the dough, then roll it around in tight circles on the countertop, to shape it into a smooth and round ball.

Step 9:
As you finish rolling each dough piece into a ball, place it on the half-sheet pan so that all 16 will fit with uniform space between each.

Step 10:
When all 16 dough balls are on the half-sheet, lightly coat the tops of the balls with non-stick cooking vegetable oil spray. Set aside. Allow dough balls to rise for 1/2 to 1 hour, until doubled in volume.

Step 11:
Preheat oven to 375 degrees.

Step 12:
With a pastry brush, gently and lightly coat each roll with butter, covering the entire visible surface.

Step 13:
Place the pan into the pre-heated oven, on the middle rack. Bake for 18 to 22 minutes, until golden-brown on top and middle of rolls register 180 degrees on your thermometer..

Step 14:
Remove the rolls from the sheet with a spatula and place these directly on a wire rack to cool.

Step 15:
Wait 5 minutes, then serve.

Fresh Storage:

Once cooled to room temperature, place rolls in a plastic sealable bag and store in the refrigerator. May reheat in the oven on a half-sheet pan uncovered or in a microwave uncovered. Use within 1 week.

Frozen Storage:

Once cooled to room temperature, place rolls in a plastic sealable bag, move to refrigerator until completely cooled, then move to freezer. Remove from freezer and place on countertop to thaw before use. May reheat in the oven on a half-sheet pan uncovered or in a microwave uncovered. May be frozen up to 1 month.

Your Notes:

_____

_____

Greek Village Bread

Ingredients:
2 & 1/4 tsp active dry yeast
1 & 1/4 cups warm water (80 to 100 degrees)
2 Tbsp honey
2 cups semolina flour
4 cups bread flour
2 Tbsp olive oil
2 Tbsp milk
1 Tbsp sugar
1/2 Tbsp salt

Directions:
Step 1:
Lightly coat half-sheet pan with non-stick cooking vegetable oil spray. Set aside.

Step 2:
In a bowl, add yeast, warm water, and honey, then mix with a spoon / spatula to combine well. Set aside for 5 minutes.

Step 3:
Add flours, oil, milk, sugar, and salt then mix with a spoon / spatula to combine well.

Step 4:
Knead for 5 minutes until smooth and pliable. **Or** put in an electric mixer with dough hook attachment and mix in the bowl for 5 minutes on medium speed, only adding a little extra flour if sticky.

Step 5:
Transfer dough to half-sheet pan.

Step 6:
Using bare hands, shape the dough into an oblong loaf 16 inches in length and of uniform thickness.

Step 7:
Lightly spritz top of dough with non-stick cooking vegetable oil spray. Set aside for 1 to 2 hours, until dough doubles in volume.

Step 8:
Preheat oven to 450 degrees.

Step 9:
Place the pan into the pre-heated oven, on the middle rack. Bake for 25 to 35 minutes, until golden-brown on top and middle of loaf registers 180 degrees on your thermometer.

Step 10:
Remove pan from the oven and use a spatula (or 2) to transfer the bread onto a wire rack.

Step 11:
Wait 10 minutes, then slice and serve.

Fresh Storage:
Once cooled to room temperature, cover the bread with plastic film / wrap or place in a plastic sealable bag and store on the countertop for up to 3 days **Or** store in the refrigerator and use within 1 week. Do not reheat.

Frozen Storage:
Once cooled to room temperature, cover the bread with plastic wrap or place in a plastic sealable bag, move to refrigerator until completely cooled, then move to freezer. Remove from freezer and place on countertop to thaw before use. May be frozen up to 1 month. Do not reheat.

Your Notes:

_____

_____

Guinness Bread

Ingredients:
4 cups bread flour
2 Tbsp baking powder
1 tsp salt
1/4 cup sugar
12 oz Guinness Extra Stout beer
2 eggs, whisked

This recipe is a quick one. It is important to have everything measured and ready to use before you begin mixing. Your reward will be a hearty bread with a hops flavor "finish".

Directions:
Step 1:
Preheat oven to 375 degrees.

Step 2:
Lightly coat inside of 5 x 9 with non-stick cooking vegetable oil spray. Set aside.

Step 3:
In a bowl, add bread flour, baking powder, salt, and sugar, then whisk to combine well.

Step 4:
Add Guinness. (If any remains in the bottle / can, then drink it or have me over for a pint!) Add eggs, then stir with a spoon / spatula, until it becomes a uniform mixture. You do not need to knead this bread - quick and easy!

Step 5:
Transfer dough to 5 x 9 inch pan by pouring the mixture then scraping the sides of the bowl with a spoon / spatula.

Step 6:
Place the pan into the pre-heated oven, on the middle rack. Bake for 70 minutes, until top is golden-brown on top and middle of loaf registers 180 degrees on your thermometer.

Step 7:
Remove pan from the oven and hold upside down over countertop to remove the breads from the pans. **Or** if the bread sticks to the pan, then stick a table-knife straight down between the edge of the pan and the bread, then "run" the knife along all the edges to trace the outline of the bread away from the pan, then hold the pan upside down again to remove the bread from the pan.

Step 8:
Transfer bread onto a wire rack, "right side" side up.

Step 9:
Wait 10 minutes, then slice and serve.

Fresh Storage:

Once cooled to room temperature, cover bread with plastic film / wrap or place in a plastic sealable bag and store in the refrigerator. Use within 1 week.

Frozen Storage:

Once cooled to room temperature, cover bread with plastic wrap or place in a plastic sealable bag, move to refrigerator until completely cooled, then move to freezer. Remove from freezer and place on countertop to thaw before use. May be frozen up to 1 month.

Your Notes:

_____

_____

Hands-Off Bread

Ingredients:
3 cups bread flour
1/4 tsp active, dry yeast
3/4 Tbsp salt
1 & 1/2 cups water (80 to 100 degrees)

Special Equipment:
Pot and lid that can go in oven such as glass, ceramic, or iron. I used the ceramic insert for a crock pot / slow cooker and placed a half-sheet pan overtop as the lid. Please ensure that your choice of pot (including the handle) and lid (including the handle) are oven-safe before use.

Variations:
You may replace 1 cup of bread flour with 1 cup of whole wheat flour, leaving just 2 cups of bread flour in the bread mixture.

Directions:
Step 1:
In a bowl, add all ingredients, then mix with a spoon or spatula until the dough begins to become one cohesive lump. The dough will not look smooth, but do not worry.

Step 2:
Cover the bowl with plastic film / wrap. Set aside on countertop at least 12 hours (but not more than 20 hours).

Step 3:
Place empty pot and lid inside oven.
Preheat oven to 450 degrees.
Once at 450 degrees, set a timer for 30 minutes.

Step 4:
After 30 minutes of pot and lid heating, remove the pot and lid and place on a heat-safe surface, such as your stovetop. Into the hot pot, gently pour the lump of dough from the bowl, using a spatula to help it release from the sides of the bowl and scraping sides of the bowl to get the entire mixture into the pot.

Step 5:
Cover pot with lid. Place the pot into the pre-heated oven, on the middle rack. Bake for 30 minutes.

Step 6:
Remove the pot and place on a heat-safe surface. Remove the lid, placing the lid on a heat safe surface, then return the uncovered pot to the oven to bake for another 15-20 minutes or until golden-brown on top and middle of loaf registers 210 degrees on your thermometer.

Step 7:
Remove the bread from the pot with a spatula and place the bread directly on a wire rack to cool.

Step 8:
Wait 5 minutes, then cut and serve.

Fresh Storage:
Once cooled to room temperature, cover the bread with plastic film / wrap and store in the refrigerator. May reheat in the oven covered with aluminum foil or in a microwave uncovered. Use within 1 week.

Frozen Storage:
Once cooled to room temperature, cover the bread with plastic wrap, move to refrigerator until completely cooled, then move to freezer. Remove from freezer and place on countertop to thaw before use. May reheat in the oven covered with aluminum foil or in a microwave uncovered. May be frozen up to 1 month.

Your Notes:

_____

_____

Honey Bread

Ingredients:
2 tsp active dry yeast
1 cup warm milk (80 to 100 degrees)
1/3 cup honey
3 Tbsp butter, melted
3 cups bread flour
1 & 1/2 tsp salt

Directions:
Step 1:
Lightly coat inside of a 5 x 9 inch loaf / bread pan with non-stick cooking vegetable oil spray. Set aside.

Step 2:
In a bowl, add yeast, milk, and honey, then mix with a spoon / spatula to combine well. Set aside for 5 minutes.

Step 3:
Add butter, flour, and salt then mix with a spoon / spatula to combine well.

Step 4:
Knead for 3 to 4 minutes until smooth and pliable. **Or** put in an electric mixer with dough hook attachment and mix in the bowl for 3 to 4 minutes on medium speed, only adding a little extra flour if sticky.

Step 5:
Using bare hands, shape the dough to fit the 5 x 9 inch pan.

Step 6:
Transfer dough to 5 x 9 inch pan.

Step 7:
Lightly spritz top of dough with non-stick cooking vegetable oil spray. Set aside for 1 to 1 & 1/2 hours, until dough doubles in volume or reaches the top of the pan.

Step 8:
Preheat oven to 350 degrees.

Step 9:
Place the pan into the pre-heated oven, on the middle rack. Bake for 40 to 45 minutes, until golden-brown on top and middle of loaf registers 180 degrees on your thermometer.

Step 10:
Remove pan from the oven and hold each one upside down over countertop to remove the bread from the pan. **Or** if the bread stick to the pan, then stick a table-knife straight down between the edge of the pan and the bread, then "run" the knife along all the edges to trace the outline of the bread away from the pan, then hold the pan upside down again to remove the bread from the pan.

Step 11:
Transfer bread onto a wire rack, "right side" side up.

Step 12:
Wait 10 minutes, then slice and serve.

Fresh Storage:
Once cooled to room temperature, cover the bread with plastic film / wrap or place in a plastic sealable bag and store on the countertop for up to 3 days **Or** store in the refrigerator and use within 1 week. Do not reheat.

Frozen Storage:
Once cooled to room temperature, cover the bread with plastic wrap or place in a plastic sealable bag, move to refrigerator until completely cooled, then move to freezer. Remove from freezer and place on countertop to thaw before use. May be frozen up to 1 month. Do not reheat.

Your Notes:

_____

_____

Naan

"nawn" (rhymes with lawn, dawn, etc)

Ingredients:
4 cups all-purpose flour
1 tsp baking powder
1 tsp salt
2 cups any plain, low-fat yogurt (dairy, Greek, soy, goat, etc.)

Variations:
Garlic Naan:
2 tsp of garlic powder
Add in Step 1, after salt.

Onion Naan:
1/4 cup of finely diced onions
Add in Step 2, after yogurt.

Garlic & Chive Naan:
2 tsp garlic powder
2 Tbsp finely chopped chives
Add both in Step 1, after salt.

Directions:
Step 1:
In a bowl, add flour, baking powder, and salt, then stir with a spoon / spatula to combine well. .

Step 2:
Add yogurt, the stir with a spoon / spatula to combine well.

Step 3:
Knead 3 to 4 minutes, until smooth and pliable. **Or** put in an electric mixer with dough hook attachment and mix in the bowl for 3 to 4 minutes on low speed, only adding a little extra flour if sticky.

Step 4:
Divide dough into 10 equal pieces.

Step 5:
Preheat a large, dry pan or griddle on medium heat.

Step 6:
Set out a dinner-size plate or serving platter. Wet a clean dish- / kitchen-towel with warm tap water, wring it out, then place it over the plate / platter.

Step 7:
For each of the 10 pieces of dough, cup your hand over the top of the dough, then roll it around in tight circles on the countertop, to shape it into a smooth and round ball. Set each aside until the 10 pieces have been made into balls.

Step 8:
On the floured countertop, with a rolling pin, roll out 1 ball into an 8 inch circle.

Step 9:
Lightly spritz hot pan with non-stick cooking vegetable oil spray, then transfer 1 dough circle to the pan, gently lowering it on 1 edge and then laying dough down flat. Fry for 1 to 2 minutes. The naan will puff up and develop nice brown spots. Using tongs, grasp 1 edge and flip over the dough circle. Fry 1 to 2 more minutes.

Step 10:
Then, using tongs, grasp 1 edge, hold the naan above the pan to allow oil to drain for a few seconds, and then stack on a plain plate or serving platter, covering the naan with the warm, damp towel.

Step 11:
Repeat Step 8 to Step 10 until all 10 naan have been made. Continue to spritz oil before each dough circle goes into the hot pan. Continue to stack and cover naan with the warm, damp towel, until ready to serve.

Fresh Storage:
Once cooled to room temperature, cover naan with plastic film / wrap or place in a plastic sealable bag and store in the refrigerator. May reheat in the oven if wrapped entirely in aluminum foil (just one or in a stack) or in a microwave uncovered. Use within 1 week.

Frozen Storage:
Once cooled to room temperature, cover naan with plastic wrap or place in a plastic sealable bag, move to refrigerator until completely cooled, then move to freezer. Remove from freezer and place on countertop to thaw before use. May reheat in the oven if wrapped entirely in aluminum foil (just one or in a stack) or in a microwave uncovered. May be frozen up to 1 month.

Your Notes:

_____

_____

Oat Bread

Ingredients:
2 tsp active dry yeast
1 & 1/4 cups warm milk (80 to 100 degrees)
3 Tbsp honey
2 Tbsp butter, softened
3 cups bread flour
1 cup rolled oats / old-fashioned oats
1 & 1/2 tsp salt

Variations:
> 3/4 cup raisins or currants
> Add in Step 4.

Directions:
Step 1:
Lightly coat inside of a 5 x 9 inch loaf / bread pan with non-stick cooking vegetable oil spray. Set aside.

Step 2:
In a bowl, add yeast, milk, and honey, then mix with a spoon / spatula to combine well. Set aside for 5 minutes.

Step 3:
Add butter, flour, oats, and salt then mix with a spoon / spatula to combine well.

Step 4:
Knead for 3 to 4 minutes until smooth and pliable. **Or** put in an electric mixer with dough hook attachment and mix in the bowl for 3 to 4 minutes on medium speed, only adding a little extra flour if sticky. During kneading / mixing, add in raisins gradually, until evenly dispersed.

Step 5:
Using bare hands, shape the dough to fit the 5 x 9 inch pan.

Step 6:
Transfer dough to 5 x 9 inch pan.

Step 7:
Lightly spritz top of dough with non-stick cooking vegetable oil spray. Set aside for 1 to 1 & 1/2 hours, until dough doubles in volume or reaches the top of the pan.

Step 8:
Preheat oven to 350 degrees.

Step 9:
Place the pan into the pre-heated oven, on the middle rack. Bake for 40 to 45 minutes, until golden-brown on top and middle of loaf registers 180 degrees on your thermometer.

Step 10:
Remove pan from the oven and hold each one upside down over countertop to remove the bread from the pan. **Or** if the bread stick to the pan, then stick a table-knife straight down between the edge of the pan and the bread, then "run" the knife along all the edges to trace the outline of the bread away from the pan, then hold the pan upside down again to remove the bread from the pan.

Step 11:
Transfer bread onto a wire rack, "right side" side up.

Step 12:
Wait 10 minutes, then slice and serve.

Fresh Storage:
Once cooled to room temperature, cover the bread with plastic film / wrap or place in a plastic sealable bag and store on the countertop for up to 3 days **Or** store in the refrigerator and use within 1 week. Do not reheat.

Frozen Storage:
Once cooled to room temperature, cover the bread with plastic wrap or place in a plastic sealable bag, move to refrigerator until completely cooled, then move to freezer. Remove from freezer and place on countertop to thaw before use. May be frozen up to 1 month. Do not reheat.

Your Notes:

_____

_____

Pizza Dough

Ingredients:
4 & 1/2 cups bread flour
1 & 1/4 tsp active dry yeast
2 cups water, chilled
1 & 3/4 tsp salt
2 Tbsp olive oil

Directions:
Step 1:
In a bowl, add flour, yeast, and water, then mix with a spoon / spatula until well combined.

Step 2:
Add salt, then mix again until well combined.

Step 3:
Cover the bowl with plastic wrap / film and transfer to refrigerator for a minimum of 8 hours. Dough can be kept waiting for up to 3 days.

Step 4:
Transfer bowl from refrigerator to countertop and set aside for 2 hours.

Step 5:
Preheat oven to 450 degrees. If you have a baking stone, preheat the stone in the oven.

Step 6:
Knead 2 to 3 minutes. Do not use a mixer. Do not clean the flour from the countertop after kneading. If the flour was used up during kneading, then reapply flour dusting to the countertop.

Step 7:
Cut dough in half.

Step 8:
Roll out 1 half-dough piece with a rolling pin until it begins to hold its shape and becomes a rectangle approximately 12 x 17 inches. Each half-dough piece will make a pizza.

Side note: Want to save the other half-dough piece for a pizza later on?
Choice 1: Transfer the half-dough piece back into the bowl and cover it with plastic wrap / film, transfer the covered bowl to the refrigerator, then keep for up to 3 days from date that you did Step 1. To use, transfer the bowl to countertop and allow to come to room temperature, then preheat oven to 450 degrees, dust flour on the countertop area, then move on to Step 6.
Choice 2: Roll out the half-dough piece as described in Step 6, transfer shaped dough to a half-sheet pan, cover pan with plastic wrap / film, transfer covered pan to freezer, then keep for up to 2 weeks from date that you did Step 1. To thaw, transfer pan to countertop, remove dough to countertop, and allow dough to come to room temperature, then preheat oven to 450 degrees, then move on to Step 7.

Step 9:
Using a pastry brush, brush olive oil on one side gently and lightly. You do not have to use all the oil. Transfer shaped dough to a half-sheet pan or baking / pizza stone, placing the oil side down.

Step 10:
Top dough with your choice of pizza toppings - get creative!

Step 11:
Place the pan / pre-heated stone into the pre-heated oven, on the middle rack. Bake for 10 to 15 minutes, until cheese is golden brown and pizza is done to your preference

Step 12:
Remove the pizza from the oven and place the pan / stone on heat-safe surface, such as stovetop.

Step 13:
Cut and serve.

Fresh Storage:
Once cooled to room temperature, cover the pizza with plastic film / wrap or place in a plastic sealable bag and store in the refrigerator. May reheat in the oven on a half-sheet pan / pizza stone uncovered. Use within 3 days.

Frozen Storage:
Once cooled to room temperature, cover the pizza with plastic wrap or place in a plastic sealable bag, move to refrigerator until completely cooled, then move to freezer. Remove from freezer and place on countertop to thaw before use. May reheat in the oven on a half-sheet pan / pizza stone uncovered. May be frozen up to 1 month.

Your Notes:

_____

_____

Pretzel Rolls / Buns

Ingredients:

1 cup warm water (80 to 100 degrees)
2 & 1/4 tsp active dry yeast
1 Tbsp sugar
2 & 3/4 cups bread flour
1 tsp salt
8 cups water
1/4 cup baking soda
1/2 tsp salt

Directions:

Step 1:
In a bowl, add warm water, yeast, and sugar, then stir with a spoon / spatula to combine. Allow to sit for 5 minutes.

Step 2:
Add flour and 1 tsp salt, then stir with a spoon / spatula to combine.

Step 3:
Knead 4 to 5 minutes, until smooth and pliable. **Or** put in an electric mixer with dough hook attachment and mix in the bowl for 4 to 5 minutes on medium speed, only adding a little extra flour if sticky.

Step 4:
Divide the dough into 8 equal pieces.

Step 5:
For each of the 8 pieces of dough, cup your hand over the top of the dough, then roll it around in tight circles on the countertop, to shape it into a smooth and round ball. Set each aside until the 8 pieces have been made into balls.

Step 6:
Lightly spritz over tops of balls with non-stick vegetable cooking oil spray. Set aside for 30 to 60 minutes, until dough balls have doubled in volume.

Step 7:
Preheat oven to 425 degrees.

Step 8:
Lightly coat a half-sheet pan with non-stick cooking vegetable oil spray. Set aside.

Step 9:
In a pot, on high heat, add 8 cups of water, until it boils.

Step 10:
To boiling water, add 1/4 cup baking soda, reduce heat to medium, and maintain to simmer.

Step 11:
Transfer 1 dough ball onto a slotted spoon, gently place the ball into the simmering water, and allow it to slide off of the slotted spoon.

Step 12:
Repeat Step 11 until 2 or 3 rolls are in the water together.

Step 13:
Simmer for 1 minute. Then using a slotted spoon, turn over the rolls, and simmer for 1 more minute.

Step 14:
With a slotted spoon, transfer the pretzel rolls one at a time onto the half-sheet pan.

Step 15:
Repeat Step 11 to Step 14, until 8 pretzel rolls are on the half-sheet pan.

Step 16:
Sprinkle 1/2 tsp salt over the 8 rolls.

Step 17:
Place the pan into the pre-heated oven, on the middle rack. Bake for 10 to 15 minutes, until golden brown on top.

Step 18:
Remove the rolls from the pan with a spatula and place these directly on a wire rack to cool.

Step 19:
Wait 5 minutes, then serve.

These pretzel rolls can be eaten as dinner rolls with a meal, or these can be sliced in half for excellent buns for sandwiches, including deli / sliced meats, veggie burgers, hamburgers, & bison burgers.

Fresh Storage:
Once cooled to room temperature, place rolls in a plastic sealable bag and store in the refrigerator. May reheat in the oven on a half-sheet pan uncovered or in a microwave uncovered. Use within 1 week.

Frozen Storage:
Once cooled to room temperature, place rolls in a plastic sealable bag, move to refrigerator until completely cooled, then move to freezer. Remove from freezer and place on countertop to thaw before use. May reheat in the oven on a half-sheet pan uncovered or in a microwave uncovered. May be frozen up to 1 month.

Your Notes:

_____

_____

Pullman Loaf Sandwich Bread: Wheat
*Special Equipment recipe using Pullman pan & lid

Ingredients:
1 Tbsp active dry yeast
1 & 1/2 cups warm water (80 to 100 degrees)
1/4 cup dry whole milk (powdered milk)
2 cups wheat flour (separated into 1 cup and 1 cups)
2 cups bread flour
6 Tbsp butter, softened
2 Tbsp honey
2 tsp salt

Special Equipment:
Pullman bread loaf pan with lid for full loaf (extra long to make traditional sandwich bread like in a store's bread aisle) **If you do not have a Pullman bread loaf pan with a lid, then please turn to the next recipe for alternate directions using 5 x 9 inch bread / loaf pans.**

Directions:
Step 1:
Lightly coat inside of Pullman loaf pan and underside of lid with non-stick cooking vegetable oil spray, then set aside.

Step 2:
In a bowl, add yeast, water, dry milk, and 1 cup of wheat flour, then mix with a spoon / spatula to combine well. Set aside for 5 minutes.

Step 3:
Add all remaining flour, then mix with a spoon / spatula to combine well.

Step 4:
Add butter, honey, and salt, then mix with a spoon / spatula to combine well.

Step 5:
Knead for 2 to 3 minutes until smooth and pliable. **Or** put in an electric mixer with dough hook attachment and mix in the bowl for 2 to 3 minutes on medium speed, only adding a little extra flour if sticky. Do not clean the flour from the countertop after kneading. If the flour was used up during kneading, then reapply flour dusting to the countertop.

Step 6:
Roll out dough to the length of the Pullman pan. Transfer dough to Pullman pan.

Step 7:
Attach the lid, but leave lid slightly open to observe the dough rising. Set aside for 1 to 1 & 1/2 hours to let rise - should be done rising when about 1/2 or 1/4 inch away from the top of the Pullman pan.

Step 8:
Preheat oven to 425 degrees.

Step 9:
Fully close the lid on the Pullman pan. Place the pan into the pre-heated oven, on the middle rack. Bake with the lid on for 30 minutes. Then, slide off the lid, and place it on a heat-safe surface. Transfer the uncovered Pullman pan back into the oven, on the middle rack, and continue baking uncovered for 30 minutes, until golden-brown on top and middle of loaf registers 180 degrees on your thermometer.

Step 10:
Remove pan from the oven and hold upside down over countertop to remove the bread from the pan. **Or** if the bread sticks to the pan, then stick a table-knife straight down between the edge of the pan and the bread, then "run" the knife along all the edges to trace the outline of the bread away from the pan, then hold the pan upside down again to remove the bread from the pan.

Step 11:
Transfer bread onto a wire rack, "right side" side up.

Step 12:
Wait 10 minutes, then slice and serve.

Fresh Storage:
Once cooled to room temperature, cover the bread with plastic film / wrap or place in a plastic sealable bag and store on the countertop for up to 3 days **Or** store in the refrigerator and use within 1 week.

Frozen Storage:
Once cooled to room temperature, cover the bread with plastic wrap or place in a plastic sealable bag, move to refrigerator until completely cooled, then move to freezer. Remove from freezer and place on countertop to thaw before use. May be frozen up to 1 month.

Your Notes:

Pullman Loaf Sandwich Bread: Wheat
*alternate recipe for 5 x 9 inch bread / loaf pans

Ingredients:
1 Tbsp active dry yeast
1 & 1/2 cups water (80 to 100 degrees)
1/4 cup dry whole milk (powdered milk)
2 cups wheat flour (separated into 1 cup and 1 cups)
2 cups bread flour
6 Tbsp butter, softened
2 Tbsp honey
2 tsp salt

Special Equipment:
If you do not have a Pullman loaf pan, then follow this recipe. If you do have a Pullman loaf pan, then please go back one recipe for alternate directions.
Or 2 of the 5 x 9 inch bread / loaf pans for making a half-loaf in each pan, for a total of a full loaf
Or divide all ingredient amounts in half to make 1 of the 5 x 9 inch bread / loaf pans for a single half-loaf

Directions:
Step 1:
Lightly coat inside of both pans with non-stick cooking vegetable oil spray. Set aside.

Step 2:
In a bowl, add yeast, water, dry milk, and 1 cup of wheat flour, then mix with a spoon / spatula to combine well. Set aside for 5 minutes.

Step 3:
Add all remaining flour, then mix with a spoon / spatula to combine well.

Step 4: Add butter, honey, and salt, then mix with a spoon / spatula to combine dough well.

Step 5:
Knead for 2 to 3 minutes until smooth and pliable. **Or** put in an electric mixer with dough hook attachment and mix in the bowl for 2 to 3 minutes on medium speed, only adding a little extra flour if sticky. Do not clean the flour from the countertop after kneading. If the flour was used up during kneading, then reapply flour dusting to the countertop.

Step 6:
Cut the dough in half. Then, roll each dough half to fit each pan. Transfer dough to 5 x 9 inch pans.

Step 7:
Lightly spritz top of dough with non-stick cooking vegetable oil spray. Set aside for 1 to 1 & 1/2 hours to let rise - should be done rising when reaches the top of the pan.

Step 8:
Preheat oven to 400 degrees.

Step 9:
Place the 2 pans into the pre-heated oven, on the middle rack, side by side. Bake for 35 minutes, golden-brown on top and middle of loaves register 180 degrees on your thermometer. **Or** if your oven bakes unevenly, then rotate the pans half-way through the baking time.

Step 10:
Remove pans from the oven and hold each one upside down over countertop to remove the breads from the pans. **Or** if the breads stick to the pans, then stick a table-knife straight down between the edge of the pans and the breads, then "run" the knife along all the edges to trace the outline of the breads away from the pans, then hold the pans upside down again to remove the breads from the pans.

Step 11:
Transfer breads onto a wire rack, "right side" side up.

Step 12:
Wait 10 minutes, then slice and serve.

Fresh Storage:
Once cooled to room temperature, cover the bread with plastic film / wrap or place in a plastic sealable bag and store on the countertop for up to 3 days **Or** store in the refrigerator and use within 1 week.

Frozen Storage:
Once cooled to room temperature, cover the bread with plastic wrap or place in a plastic sealable bag, move to refrigerator until completely cooled, then move to freezer. Remove from freezer and place on countertop to thaw before use. May be frozen up to 1 month.

Your Notes:

_____

_____

Pullman Loaf Sandwich Bread: White
*Special Equipment recipe using Pullman pan & lid

Ingredients:
1 Tbsp active dry yeast
1 & 1/2 cups warm water (80 to 100 degrees)
1/4 cup dry whole milk (powdered milk)
4 cups bread flour (separated into 1 cup and 3 cups)
6 Tbsp butter, softened
2 Tbsp honey
2 tsp salt

Special Equipment:
Pullman bread loaf pan with lid for full loaf (extra long to make traditional sandwich bread like in a store's bread aisle)
If you do not have a Pullman bread loaf pan with a lid, then please turn to the next recipe for alternate directions using 5 x 9 inch bread / loaf pans.

Directions:
Step 1:
Lightly coat inside of Pullman loaf pan and underside of lid with non-stick cooking vegetable oil spray, then set aside.

Step 2:
In a bowl, add yeast, water, dry milk, and 1 cup of flour, then mix with a spoon / spatula to combine well. Set aside for 5 minutes.

Step 3:
Add remaining flour, then mix with a spoon / spatula to combine well.

Step 4:
Add butter, honey, and salt, then mix with a spoon / spatula to combine well.

Step 5:
Knead for 2 to 3 minutes until smooth and pliable. **Or** put in an electric mixer with dough hook attachment and mix in the bowl for 2 to 3 minutes on medium speed, only adding a little extra flour if sticky. Do not clean the flour from the countertop after kneading. If the flour was used up during kneading, then reapply flour dusting to the countertop.

Step 6:
Roll out dough to the length of the Pullman pan. Transfer dough to Pullman pan.

Step 7:
Attach the lid, but leave lid slightly open to observe the dough rising. Set aside for 1 to 1 & 1/2 hours to let rise - should be done rising when about 1/2 or 1/4 inch away from the top of the Pullman pan.

Step 8:
Preheat oven to 425 degrees.

Step 9:
Fully close the lid on the Pullman pan. Place the pan into the pre-heated oven, on the middle rack. Bake with the lid on for 30 minutes. Then, slide off the lid, and place it on a heat-safe surface. Transfer the uncovered Pullman pan back into the oven, on the middle rack, and continue baking uncovered for 30 minutes, until golden-brown on top and middle of loaf registers 180 degrees on your thermometer.

Step 10:
Remove pan from the oven and hold upside down over countertop to remove the bread from the pan. **Or** if the bread sticks to the pan, then stick a table-knife straight down between the edge of the pan and the bread, then "run" the knife along all the edges to trace the outline of the bread away from the pan, then hold the pan upside down again to remove the bread from the pan.

Step 11:
Transfer bread onto a wire rack, "right side" side up.

Step 12:
Wait 10 minutes, then slice and serve.

Fresh Storage:
Once cooled to room temperature, cover the bread with plastic film / wrap or place in a plastic sealable bag and store on the countertop for up to 3 days **Or** store in the refrigerator and use within 1 week.

Frozen Storage:
Once cooled to room temperature, cover the bread with plastic wrap or place in a plastic sealable bag, move to refrigerator until completely cooled, then move to freezer. Remove from freezer and place on countertop to thaw before use. May be frozen up to 1 month.

Your Notes:

_____

_____

Pullman Loaf Sandwich Bread: White
*alternate recipe for 5 x 9 inch bread / loaf pans

Ingredients:
1 Tbsp active dry yeast
1 & 1/2 cups warm water (80 to 100 degrees)
1/4 cup dry whole milk (powdered milk)
4 cups bread flour (separated into 1 cup and 3 cups)
6 Tbsp butter, softened
2 Tbsp honey
2 tsp salt

Special Equipment:
If you do not have a Pullman loaf pan, then follow this recipe. If you do have a Pullman loaf pan, then please go back one recipe for alternate directions.
Or 2 of the 5 x 9 inch bread / loaf pans for making a half-loaf in each pan, for a total of a full loaf
Or divide all ingredient amounts in half to make 1 of the 5 x 9 inch bread / loaf pans for a single half-loaf

Directions:
Step 1:
Lightly coat inside of both pans with non-stick cooking vegetable oil spray. Set aside.

Step 2:
In a bowl, add yeast, water, dry milk, and 1 cup of flour, then mix with a spoon / spatula to combine well. Set aside for 5 minutes.

Step 3:
Add remaining flour, then mix with a spoon / spatula to combine well.

Step 4:
Add butter, honey, and salt, then mix with a spoon / spatula to combine well.

Step 5:
Knead for 2 to 3 minutes until smooth and pliable. **Or** put in an electric mixer with dough hook attachment and mix in the bowl for 2 to 3 minutes on medium speed, only adding a little extra flour if sticky. Do not clean the flour from the countertop after kneading. If the flour was used up during kneading, then reapply flour dusting to the countertop.

Step 6:
Cut the dough in half. Then, roll each dough half to fit each pan. Transfer dough to 5 x 9 inch pans.

Step 7:
Lightly spritz top of dough with non-stick cooking vegetable oil spray. Set aside for 1 to 1 & 1/2 hours to let rise - should be done rising when reaches the top of the pan.

Step 8:
Preheat oven to 400 degrees.

Step 9:
Place the 2 pans into the pre-heated oven, on the middle rack, side by side. Bake for 35 minutes, until golden-brown on top and middle of loaves register 180 degrees on your thermometer. **Or** if your oven bakes unevenly, then rotate the pans half-way through the baking time.

Step 10:
Remove pans from the oven and hold each one upside down over countertop to remove the breads from the pans. **Or** if the breads stick to the pans, then stick a table-knife straight down between the edge of the pans and the breads, then "run" the knife along all the edges to trace the outline of the breads away from the pans, then hold the pans upside down again to remove the breads from the pans.

Step 11:
Transfer breads onto a wire rack, "right side" side up.

Step 12:
Wait 10 minutes, then slice and serve.

Fresh Storage:
Once cooled to room temperature, cover the bread with plastic film / wrap or place in a plastic sealable bag and store on the countertop for up to 3 days **Or** store in the refrigerator and use within 1 week.

Frozen Storage:
Once cooled to room temperature, cover the bread with plastic wrap or place in a plastic sealable bag, move to refrigerator until completely cooled, then move to freezer. Remove from freezer and place on countertop to thaw before use. May be frozen up to 1 month.

Your Notes:

_____

_____

Pullman Loaf Sandwich Bread: Rye
*Special Equipment recipe using Pullman pan & lid

Ingredients:
1 Tbsp active dry yeast
1 & 1/2 cups warm buttermilk (80 to 100 degrees)
2 cups rye flour (separated into 1 cup and 1 cups)
2 cups bread flour
6 Tbsp butter, softened
2 Tbsp honey
2 tsp salt

Special Equipment:
Pullman bread loaf pan with lid for full loaf (extra long to make traditional sandwich bread like in a store's bread aisle)
If you do not have a Pullman bread loaf pan with a lid, then please turn to the next recipe for alternate directions using 5 x 9 inch bread / loaf pans.

Directions:
Step 1:
Lightly coat inside of Pullman loaf pan and underside of lid with non-stick cooking vegetable oil spray, then set aside.

Step 2:
In a bowl, add yeast, buttermilk, and 1 cup of rye flour, then mix with a spoon / spatula to combine well. Set aside for 5 minutes.

Step 3:
Add all remaining flour, then mix with a spoon / spatula to combine well.

Step 4:
Add butter, honey, and salt, then mix with a spoon / spatula to combine well.

Step 5:
Knead for 2 to 3 minutes until smooth and pliable. **Or** put in an electric mixer with dough hook attachment and mix in the bowl for 2 to 3 minutes on medium speed, only adding a little extra flour if sticky. Do not clean the flour from the countertop after kneading. If the flour was used up during kneading, then reapply flour dusting to the countertop.

Step 6:
Roll out dough to the length of the Pullman pan. Transfer dough to Pullman pan.

Step 7:
Attach the lid, but leave lid slightly open to observe the dough rising. Set aside for 1 to 1 & 1/2 hours to let rise - should be done rising when about 1/2 or 1/4 inch away from the top of the Pullman pan.

Step 8:
Preheat oven to 425 degrees.

Step 9:
Fully close the lid on the Pullman pan. Place the pan into the pre-heated oven, on the middle rack. Bake with the lid on for 30 minutes. Then, slide off the lid, and place it on a heat-safe surface. Transfer the uncovered Pullman pan back into the oven, on the middle rack, and continue baking uncovered for 30 minutes, until golden-brown on top and middle of loaf registers 180 degrees on your thermometer.

Step 10:
Remove pan from the oven and hold upside down over countertop to remove the bread from the pan. **Or** if the bread sticks to the pan, then stick a table-knife straight down between the edge of the pan and the bread, then "run" the knife along all the edges to trace the outline of the bread away from the pan, then hold the pan upside down again to remove the bread from the pan.

Step 11:
Transfer bread onto a wire rack, "right side" side up.

Step 12:
Wait 10 minutes, then slice and serve.

Fresh Storage:
Once cooled to room temperature, cover the bread with plastic film / wrap or place in a plastic sealable bag and store on the countertop for up to 3 days **Or** store in the refrigerator and use within 1 week.

Frozen Storage:
Once cooled to room temperature, cover the bread with plastic wrap or place in a plastic sealable bag, move to refrigerator until completely cooled, then move to freezer. Remove from freezer and place on countertop to thaw before use. May be frozen up to 1 month.

Your Notes:

_____

_____

Pullman Loaf Sandwich Bread: Rye
*alternate recipe for 5 x 9 inch bread / loaf pans

Ingredients:
1 Tbsp active dry yeast
1 & 1/2 cups warm buttermilk (80 to 100 degrees)
2 cups rye flour (separated into 1 cup and 1 cups)
2 cups bread flour
6 Tbsp butter, softened
2 Tbsp honey
2 tsp salt

Special Equipment:
If you do not have a Pullman loaf pan, then follow this recipe. If you do have a Pullman loaf pan, then please go back one recipe for alternate directions.
Or 2 of the 5 x 9 inch bread / loaf pans for making a half-loaf in each pan, for a total of a full loaf
Or divide all ingredient amounts in half to make 1 of the 5 x 9 inch bread / loaf pans for a single half-loaf

Directions:
Step 1:
Lightly coat inside of both pans with non-stick cooking vegetable oil spray. Set aside.

Step 2:
In a bowl, add yeast, buttermilk, and 1 cup of rye flour, then mix with a spoon / spatula to combine well. Set aside for 5 minutes.

Step 3:
Add all remaining flour, then mix with a spoon / spatula to combine well.

Step 4:
Add butter, honey, and salt, then mix with a spoon / spatula to combine well.

Step 5:
Knead for 2 to 3 minutes until smooth and pliable. **Or** put in an electric mixer with dough hook attachment and mix in the bowl for 2 to 3 minutes on medium speed, only adding a little extra flour if sticky. Do not clean the flour from the countertop after kneading. If the flour was used up during kneading, then reapply flour dusting to the countertop.

Step 6:
Cut the dough in half. Then, roll each dough half to fit each pan. Transfer dough to 5 x 9 inch pans.

Step 7:
Lightly spritz top of dough with non-stick cooking vegetable oil spray. Set aside for 1 to 1 & 1/2 hours to let rise - should be done rising when reaches the top of the pan.

Step 8:
Preheat oven to 400 degrees.

Step 9:
Place the 2 pans into the pre-heated oven, on the middle rack, side by side. Bake for 35 minutes, until golden-brown on top and middle of loaves register 180 degrees on your thermometer. **Or** if your oven bakes unevenly, then rotate the pans half-way through the baking time.

Step 10:
Remove pans from the oven and hold each one upside down over countertop to remove the breads from the pans. **Or** if the breads stick to the pans, then stick a table-knife straight down between the edge of the pans and the breads, then "run" the knife along all the edges to trace the outline of the breads away from the pans, then hold the pans upside down again to remove the breads from the pans.

Step 11:
Transfer breads onto a wire rack, "right side" side up.

Step 12:
Wait 10 minutes, then slice and serve.

Fresh Storage:
Once cooled to room temperature, cover the bread with plastic film / wrap or place in a plastic sealable bag and store on the countertop for up to 3 days **Or** store in the refrigerator and use within 1 week.

Frozen Storage:
Once cooled to room temperature, cover the bread with plastic wrap or place in a plastic sealable bag, move to refrigerator until completely cooled, then move to freezer. Remove from freezer and place on countertop to thaw before use. May be frozen up to 1 month.

Your Notes:

_____

_____

Pumpkin Bread

Ingredients:
3 cups sugar
1/2 cup vegetable oil
1/ 2 cup butter, melted
3 eggs, whisked
16 oz canned pumpkin
3 cups all-purpose flour
1 tsp ground cloves
1 tsp ground cinnamon
1 tsp ground nutmeg
1 tsp baking soda
1/2 tsp salt
1/2 tsp baking powder

Variations:
1 cup walnuts, chopped
Add in Step 5 & 3/4

Directions:
Step 1:
Preheat oven to 350 degrees.

Step 2:
Lightly coat inside of 2 5 x 9 loaf / bread pans with non-stick cooking vegetable oil spray. Set aside.

Step 3:
In a bowl, add sugar and oil, then stir with a spoon / spatula to combine well.

Step 4:
Add eggs and pumpkin, then stir with a spoon / spatula to combine well.

Step 5:
Add flour, cloves, cinnamon, nutmeg, baking soda, salt, and baking powder, then stir with a spoon / spatula to combine well. Make sure that the dry and wet ingredients are fully combined by scraping the bottom of the mixing bowl several times to make sure there are no pockets of flour. The dough may look soupy.

Step 5 & 3/4:
Optional: Add nuts, then gently stir with a spoon / spatula a few times.

Step 6:
Transfer dough equally between 2 5 x 9 inch pans by pouring the mixture, then scraping the sides of the bowl with a spoon / spatula.

Step 7:
Smooth tops of doughs with spoon / spatula.

Step 8:
Place the pans into the pre-heated oven, on the middle rack, side by side. Bake for 70 minutes, until middle of loaves register 180 degrees on your thermometer.

Step 9:
Remove pans from the oven and place on a wire cooling rack for 10 minutes.

Step 10:
Hold pans upside down over countertop to remove the breads from the pans. **Or** if the bread sticks to the pan, then stick a table-knife straight down between the edge of the pans and the breads, then "run" the knife along all the edges to trace the outline of the breads away from the pans, then hold the pans upside down again to remove the breads from the pans.

Step 11:
Transfer breads onto a wire rack, "right side" side up.

Step 12:
Wait 5 minutes, then slice and serve.

Fresh Storage:
Once cooled to room temperature, cover bread with plastic film / wrap or place in a plastic sealable bag and store in the refrigerator. Use within 1 week. Do not reheat.

Frozen Storage:
Once cooled to room temperature, cover bread with plastic wrap or place in a plastic sealable bag, move to refrigerator until completely cooled, then move to freezer. Remove from freezer and place on countertop to thaw before use. May be frozen up to 1 month. Do not reheat.

Your Notes:

_____

_____

Rosemary Rolls

Ingredients:
1/4 cup olive oil
1 Tbsp fresh rosemary, stems removed and leaves chopped
2 & 1/4 tsp active dry yeast
1 cup water (80 to 100 degrees)
3 & 1/4 cups bread flour (separated into 1/2 cup and
                    2 & 3/4 cups)
1 & 3/4 tsp salt
1/4 cup butter, melted then cooled for a few minutes

Directions:
Step 1:
Lightly coat a half-sheet pan with non-stick cooking
vegetable oil spray. Set aside.

Step 2:
In a bowl, add olive oil and rosemary, then set aside on the
countertop to marinate for at least 30 minutes.

Step 3:
In another bowl, add yeast, water, and 1/2 cup of flour, then
mix with a spoon / spatula to combine well. Set aside for 5
minutes to give yeast a chance to begin working.

Step 4:
Add remaining flour, then mix with a spoon / spatula to
combine well.

Step 5:
Add salt and rosemary/olive oil, then mix with a spoon /
spatula to combine well.

Step 6:
Knead for 2 to 3 minutes until smooth and pliable. **Or** put in an electric mixer with dough hook attachment and mix in the bowl for 2 to 3 minutes on medium speed, only adding a little extra flour if sticky. Do not clean the flour from the countertop after kneading. If the flour was used up during kneading, then reapply flour dusting to the countertop.

Step 7:
Cut dough in half. Then, cut each half into half again. Then, cut each quarter in half again, for a total of 8 pieces of dough.

Step 8:
For each of the 8 pieces of dough, cup your hand over the top of the dough, then roll it around in tight circles on the countertop, to shape it into a smooth and round ball.

Step 9:
As you finish rolling each dough piece into a ball, place it on the half-sheet pan so that all 8 will fit with uniform space between each.

Step 10:
When all 8 dough balls are on the half-sheet, lightly coat the tops of the balls with non-stick cooking vegetable oil spray. Set aside. Allow dough balls to rise for 1 hour, until doubled in volume.

Step 10:
Preheat oven to 450 degrees.

Step 11:
With a pastry brush, gently and lightly coat each roll with butter, covering the entire visible surface.

Step 12:
Place the pan into the pre-heated oven, on the middle rack. Bake for 10 minutes.

Step 13:
Reduce oven heat to 375 degrees. Bake for another 12 to 20 minutes, until golden-brown on top and middle of rolls registers 180 degrees on your thermometer.

Step 14:
Remove the rolls from the pan with a spatula and place these directly on a wire rack to cool.

Step 15:
Wait 5 minutes, then serve.

Fresh Storage:
Once cooled to room temperature, place rolls in a plastic sealable bag and store in the refrigerator. May reheat in the oven on a half-sheet pan uncovered or in a microwave uncovered. Use within 1 week.

Frozen Storage:
Once cooled to room temperature, place rolls in a plastic sealable bag, move to refrigerator until completely cooled, then move to freezer. Remove from freezer and place on countertop to thaw before use. May reheat in the oven on a half-sheet pan uncovered or in a microwave uncovered. May be frozen up to 1 month.

Your Notes:

_____

_____

Sausage Bread

Ingredients:
1 lb breakfast sausage
1/2 yellow onion, diced
2 eggs, beaten
1 cup mozzarella, shredded
3 cups bread flour
2 Tbsp butter, softened
1 tsp sugar
2 & 1/4 tsp active dry yeast
1 cup warm water (80 to 100 degrees)
1 & 1/4 tsp salt
1 Tbsp butter, melted

Directions:
Step 1:
Lightly coat a half-sheet pan with non-stick cooking vegetable oil spray. Set aside.

Step 2:
In a pan, on medium heat, add sausage and onion, then sauté until cooked through, stirring occasionally with a spoon / spatula.

Step 3:
Add eggs and cheese, then stir with a spoon / spatula to combine well.

Step 4:
Immediately, remove pan from heat and place on a heat-safe surface (such as a cold burner). Let mixture "cook" with residual heat. Everything will continue to cook inside the bread later. Set aside.

Step 5:
In a bowl, combine flour, 2 Tbsp butter, sugar, yeast, and water, then stir with a spoon / spatula to combine well.

Step 6:
Add salt , then stir with a spoon / spatula to combine well.

Step 7:
Knead for 3 minutes, until dough is smooth and pliable. **Or** put in an electric mixer with dough hook attachment and mix in the bowl for 3 to 4 minutes on medium speed, only adding a little extra flour if sticky. Do not clean the flour from the countertop after kneading. If the flour was used up during kneading, then reapply flour dusting to the countertop.

Step 8:
With a rolling pin, roll dough into a 10 inch x 16 inch rectangle.

Step 9:
Transfer mixture from pan onto rectangle. Spread mixture evenly, except leaving a plain 1/2 inch border along the edges of the rectangle.

Step 10:
With a 16 inch side closest to you, lift the edge and fold up and over an inch. Continue tightly rolling rectangle all the way across. Then, along the 16 inch edge, using bare hands, pinch the edge of the dough with the rolled dough to keep it from unrolling. This makes a "seam", as in sewing fabric.

Step 11:
At each exposed end of the rolled dough, using bare hands, pinch the dough together top edge to bottom edge. Flip / fold the pinched edges up toward the end of the "seam".

Step 12:
Using bare hands, gently and carefully pick up the rolled dough, turn it in your hands half way around so that the "seam" is underneath, and then lay it on the half-sheet pan.

Step 13:
Set aside 30 to 60 minutes, until doubled in volume.

Step 14:
Preheat oven to 350 degrees.

Step 15:
Place the pan into the pre-heated oven, on the middle rack. Bake for 20 minutes.

Step 16:
Remove pan to heat-safe surface. With a pastry brush, gently and lightly coat with 1 Tbsp butter, covering the entire visible surface. Transfer pan back into oven. Bake 20 to 25 minutes longer, until lightly browned on top and middle of rolled loaf registers 180 degrees on your thermometer..

Step 17:
Remove the rolled loaf from the sheet with a spatula and place directly on a wire rack to cool.

Step 18:
Wait 10 minutes, then serve slice and warm.

Fresh Storage:
Once cooled to room temperature, place rolled loaf in a plastic sealable bag and store in the refrigerator. May reheat in the oven on a half-sheet pan uncovered or in a microwave uncovered. Use within 3 days.

Frozen Storage:
Once cooled to room temperature, place rolled loaf in a plastic sealable bag, move to refrigerator until completely cooled, then move to freezer. Remove from freezer and place on countertop to thaw before use. May reheat in the oven on a half-sheet pan uncovered or in a microwave uncovered. May be frozen up to 1 month.

Your Notes:

_____

_____

Scones: Basic

Ingredients:
4 cups all-purpose flour
1/2 cup sugar
1 tsp baking soda
1 Tbsp baking powder
1/2 tsp salt
1/2 pound butter
2 eggs, whisked
1 Tbsp vanilla
2 cups buttermilk
1 cup frozen/fresh fruit of your choice

Directions:
Step1:
The secret to scones is very, very cold dairy ingredients. Once measured out, place the buttermilk in the freezer. Once measured out, cut butter into small pieces (the smaller the better) and place in a dish, then place dish in the freezer, uncovered. Leave in the freezer for at least 15 minutes and only remove when ready to use.

Step 2:
Preheat oven to 375 degrees.

Step 3:
Set out 2 half-sheet pans. Cover each pan with a piece of parchment paper. Set aside.

Step 4:
In a bowl, add eggs and vanilla, then whisk to combine well.
Set aside.

Step 5:
In a bowl, add flour, sugar, baking soda, baking powder, and
salt, then whisk to combine well.

Step 6:
To dry ingredients bowl, add very cold butter pieces. With
bare hands, coat butter pieces a little bit with dry mixture,
then begin breaking up butter with a motion similar to
snapping your fingers with your thumb moving across all
fingers, while you mix the butter more with the dry mixture,
until the dough is mealy and gritty in appearance and texture
(no pieces bigger than pea-sized). Rub hands together to
remove any mix that sticks to them.

Step 7:
To dry ingredients bowl, add egg mixture and very cold
buttermilk, then use a spatula to stir until just lightly
combined.

Important: Once the liquids are added, get the scones in the
oven as soon as possible. Do the next steps quickly.

Step 8:
Using bare hands, grab a chunk of dough that is roughly 1/3
cup and place chunk onto 1 of the parchment paper-lined
half-sheet pans so that 4-6 dough chunks will fit on each pan
with at least 2 inches of uniform spacing.

Step 9:
Repeat Step 8 for all remaining dough. These dough chunks will become scones of approximately 4 inches.

Step 10:
Place the pans side by side into the pre-heated oven, on the middle rack. Bake for 8 minutes.

Step 11:
Rotate pans. Bake for 8 to 12 more minutes. Insert a toothpick straight down into the top of the scone, until approximately in the center, then pulled straight back out to see if any dough is sticking to it or if it is "clean". If not clean, then leave pans in the oven for another minute and check again. Check/Recheck until clean.

Step 12:
Remove the pans and place directly on a wire rack to cool.

Step 13:
Wait 5 minutes, then serve.

Fresh Storage:

Once cooled to room temperature, cover scones with plastic film / wrap or place in a plastic sealable bag and store in the refrigerator. May reheat in the oven on a half-sheet pan uncovered or in a microwave uncovered. Use within 1 week.

Frozen Storage:

Once cooled to room temperature, cover scones with plastic wrap or place in a plastic sealable bag, move to refrigerator until completely cooled, then move to freezer. Remove from freezer and place on countertop to thaw before use. May reheat in the oven on a half-sheet pan uncovered or in a microwave uncovered. May be frozen up to 1 month.

Your Notes:

_____

_____

Scones: Apple Awesomeness

Ingredients:
4 cups all-purpose flour
1/2 cup sugar
1 tsp baking soda
1 Tbsp baking powder
1/2 tsp salt
1/4 cup brown sugar
1 & 1/2 Tbsp ground cinnamon
1/2 pound butter
2 eggs, whisked
1 Tbsp vanilla
2 cups buttermilk
2 cups fresh apples, peeled, cored, and diced into 1/4" bits
1 cup cinnamon baking chips

Directions:
Step1:
The secret to scones is very, very cold dairy ingredients. Once measured out, place the buttermilk in the freezer. Once measured out, cut butter into small pieces (the smaller the better) and place in a dish, then place dish in the freezer, uncovered. Leave in the freezer for at least 15 minutes and only remove when ready to use.

Step 2:
Preheat oven to 375 degrees.

Step 3:
Set out 2 half-sheet pans. Cover each pan with a piece of parchment paper. Set aside.

Step 4:
In a bowl, add eggs and vanilla, then whisk to combine well. Set aside.

Step 5:
In a bowl, add flour, sugar, baking soda, baking powder, salt, brown sugar, and cinnamon, then whisk to combine well.

Step 6:
To dry ingredients bowl, add very cold butter pieces. With bare hands, coat butter pieces a little bit with dry mixture, then begin breaking up butter with a motion similar to snapping your fingers with your thumb moving across all fingers, while you mix the butter more with the dry mixture, until the dough is mealy and gritty in appearance and texture (no pieces bigger than pea-sized). Rub hands together to remove any mix that sticks to them.

Step 7:
To dry ingredients bowl, add egg mixture and very cold buttermilk, then use a spatula to stir until lightly combined.

Step 8:
Add diced apple bits and cinnamon baking chips, then use a spatula to stir until well dispersed in dough.

Important: Once the liquids are added, get the scones in the oven as soon as possible. Do the next steps quickly.

Step 9:
Using bare hands, grab a chunk of dough that is roughly 1/3 cup and place chunk onto 1 of the parchment paper-lined half-sheet pans so that 4-6 dough chunks will fit on each pan with at least 2 inches of uniform spacing.

Step 10:
Repeat Step 9 for all remaining dough. These dough chunks will become scones of approximately 4 inches.

Step 11:
Place the pans side by side into the pre-heated oven, on the middle rack. Bake for 8 minutes.

Step 12:
Rotate pans. Bake for 8 to 12 more minutes. Insert a toothpick straight down into the top of the scone, until approximately in the center, then pulled straight back out to see if any dough is sticking to it or if it is "clean". If not clean, then leave pans in the oven for another minute and check again. Check/Recheck until clean.

Step 13:
Remove the pans and place directly on a wire rack to cool.

Step 14:
Wait 5 minutes, then serve.

Fresh Storage:

Once cooled to room temperature, cover scones with plastic film / wrap or place in a plastic sealable bag and store in the refrigerator. May reheat in the oven on a half-sheet pan uncovered or in a microwave uncovered. Use within 1 week.

Frozen Storage:

Once cooled to room temperature, cover scones with plastic wrap or place in a plastic sealable bag, move to refrigerator until completely cooled, then move to freezer. Remove from freezer and place on countertop to thaw before use. May reheat in the oven on a half-sheet pan uncovered or in a microwave uncovered. May be frozen up to 1 month.

Your Notes:

_____

_____

Scones: Blueberry & Orange

Ingredients:
4 cups all-purpose flour
1/2 cup sugar
1 tsp baking soda
1 Tbsp baking powder
1/2 tsp salt
zest of 2 oranges
1/2 pound butter
2 eggs, whisked
1 Tbsp vanilla
2 cups buttermilk
1 cup frozen blueberries
1 Tbsp orange juice
1/2 cup confectioners' sugar

Directions:
Step1:
The secret to scones is very, very cold dairy ingredients. Once measured out, place the buttermilk in the freezer. Once measured out, cut butter into small pieces (the smaller the better) and place in a dish, then place dish in the freezer, uncovered. Leave in the freezer for at least 15 minutes and only remove when ready to use.

Step 2:
Preheat oven to 375 degrees.

Step 3:
Set out 2 half-sheet pans. Cover each pan with a piece of parchment paper. Set aside.

Step 4:
In a bowl, add eggs and vanilla, then whisk to combine well. Set aside.

Step 5:
In a bowl, add flour, sugar, baking soda, baking powder, salt, and orange zest, then whisk to combine well.

Step 6:
To dry ingredients bowl, add very cold butter pieces. With bare hands, coat butter pieces a little bit with dry mixture, then begin breaking up butter with a motion similar to snapping your fingers with your thumb moving across all fingers, while you mix the butter more with the dry mixture, until the dough is mealy and gritty in appearance and texture (no pieces bigger than pea-sized). Rub hands together to remove any mix that sticks to them.

Step 7:
To dry ingredients bowl, add egg mixture and very cold buttermilk, then use a spatula to stir until lightly combined.

Step 8:
Add blueberries, then use a spatula to stir gently to avoid staining the dough.

Important: Once the liquids are added, get the scones in the oven as soon as possible. Do the next steps quickly.

Step 9:
Using bare hands, grab a chunk of dough that is roughly 1/3 cup and place chunk onto 1 of the parchment paper-lined half-sheet pans so that 4-6 dough chunks will fit on each pan with at least 2 inches of uniform spacing.

Step 10:
Repeat Step 9 for all remaining dough. These dough chunks will become scones of approximately 4 inches.

Step 11:
Place the pans side by side into the pre-heated oven, on the middle rack. Bake for 8 minutes.

Step 12:
Rotate pans. Bake for 8 to 12 more minutes. Insert a toothpick straight down into the top of the scone, until approximately in the center, then pulled straight back out to see if any dough is sticking to it or if it is "clean". If not clean, then leave pans in the oven for another minute and check again. Check/Recheck until clean.

Step 13:
Remove the pans and place directly on a wire rack to cool. Set aside to cool for 5 minutes.

Step 14:
In a bowl, add orange juice and confectioner's sugar, then whisk to combine well.

Step 15:
With a pastry brush, gently glaze the visible surface of each scone, then serve.

Fresh Storage:
Once cooled to room temperature, cover scones with plastic film / wrap or place in a plastic sealable bag and store in the refrigerator. May reheat in the oven on a half-sheet pan uncovered or in a microwave uncovered. Use within 1 week.

Frozen Storage:
Once cooled to room temperature, cover scones with plastic wrap or place in a plastic sealable bag, move to refrigerator until completely cooled, then move to freezer. Remove from freezer and place on countertop to thaw before use. May reheat in the oven on a half-sheet pan uncovered or in a microwave uncovered. May be frozen up to 1 month.

Your Notes:

_____

_____

Scones: Lemon & Candied Ginger

Ingredients:
4 cups all-purpose flour
1/2 cup sugar
1 tsp baking soda
1 Tbsp baking powder
1/2 tsp salt
1 Tbsp candied ginger
1/2 pound butter
2 eggs, whisked
2 tsp vanilla
juice of 1/2 lemon
2 cups buttermilk
1 cup frozen blueberries
zest of 2 lemons
1 Tbsp lemon juice
1/2 cup confectioners' sugar

Directions:
Step1:
The secret to scones is very, very cold dairy ingredients. Once measured out, place the buttermilk in the freezer. Once measured out, cut butter into small pieces (the smaller the better) and place in a dish, then place dish in the freezer, uncovered. Leave in the freezer for at least 15 minutes and only remove when ready to use.

Step 2:
Preheat oven to 375 degrees.

Step 3:
Set out 2 half-sheet pans. Cover each pan with a piece of parchment paper. Set aside.

Step 4:
In a bowl, add eggs, vanilla, and juice of 1/2 lemon, then whisk to combine well. Set aside.

Step 5:
In a bowl, add flour, sugar, baking soda, baking powder, salt, and lemon zest, then whisk to combine well.

Step 6:
To dry ingredients bowl, add very cold butter pieces and minced candied ginger. With bare hands, coat butter pieces and minced candied ginger bits a little bit with dry mixture, then begin breaking up butter and candied ginger with a motion similar to snapping your fingers with your thumb moving across all fingers, while you mix the butter and candied ginger more with the dry mixture, until the dough is mealy and gritty in appearance and texture (no pieces bigger than pea-sized). Ensure that candied ginger bits are evenly dispersed throughout the mixture. Rub hands together to remove any mix that sticks to them.

Step 7:
To dry ingredients bowl, add egg mixture and very cold buttermilk, then use a spatula to stir until lightly combined.

Important: Once the liquids are added, get the scones in the oven as soon as possible. Do the next steps quickly.

Step 8:
Using bare hands, grab a chunk of dough that is roughly 1/3 cup and place chunk onto 1 of the parchment paper-lined half-sheet pans so that 4-6 dough chunks will fit on each pan with at least 2 inches of uniform spacing.

Step 9:
Repeat Step 8 for all remaining dough. These dough chunks will become scones of approximately 4 inches.

Step 10:
Place the pans side by side into the pre-heated oven, on the middle rack. Bake for 8 minutes.

Step 11:
Rotate pans. Bake for 8 to 12 more minutes. Insert a toothpick straight down into the top of the scone, until approximately in the center, then pulled straight back out to see if any dough is sticking to it or if it is "clean". If not clean, then leave pans in the oven for another minute and check again. Check/Recheck until clean.

Step 12:
Remove the pans and place directly on a wire rack to cool. Set aside to cool for 5 minutes.

Step 13:
In a bowl, add 1 Tbsp lemon juice and confectioner's sugar, then whisk to combine well.

Step 14:
With a pastry brush, gently glaze the visible surface of each scone, then serve.

Fresh Storage:
Once cooled to room temperature, cover scones with plastic film / wrap or place in a plastic sealable bag and store in the refrigerator. May reheat in the oven on a half-sheet pan uncovered or in a microwave uncovered. Use within 1 week.

Frozen Storage:
Once cooled to room temperature, cover scones with plastic wrap or place in a plastic sealable bag, move to refrigerator until completely cooled, then move to freezer. Remove from freezer and place on countertop to thaw before use. May reheat in the oven on a half-sheet pan uncovered or in a microwave uncovered. May be frozen up to 1 month.

Your Notes:

_____

_____

Scones: Raspberry & White Chocolate

Ingredients:
4 cups all-purpose flour
1/2 cup sugar
1 tsp baking soda
1 Tbsp baking powder
1/2 tsp salt
1/2 pound butter
2 eggs, whisked
1 Tbsp vanilla
2 cups buttermilk
1 cup frozen red raspberries
8 oz white chocolate chips

Directions:
Step1:
The secret to scones is very, very cold dairy ingredients.
Once measured out, place the buttermilk in the freezer.
Once measured out, cut butter into small pieces (the smaller
the better) and place in a dish, then place dish in the freezer,
uncovered. Leave in the freezer for at least 15 minutes and
only remove when ready to use.

Step 2:
Preheat oven to 375 degrees.

Step 3:
Set out 2 half-sheet pans. Cover each pan with a piece of
parchment paper. Set aside.

Step 4:
In a bowl, add eggs and vanilla, then whisk to combine well. Set aside.

Step 5:
In a bowl, add flour, sugar, baking soda, baking powder, and salt, then whisk to combine well.

Step 6:
To dry ingredients bowl, add very cold butter pieces. With bare hands, coat butter pieces a little bit with dry mixture, then begin breaking up butter with a motion similar to snapping your fingers with your thumb moving across all fingers, while you mix the butter more with the dry mixture, until the dough is mealy and gritty in appearance and texture (no pieces bigger than pea-sized). Rub hands together to remove any mix that sticks to them.

Step 7:
To dry ingredients bowl, add egg mixture and very cold buttermilk, then use a spatula to stir until lightly combined.

Step 8:
Add berries and chips, then use a spatula to stir gently.

Important: Once the liquids are added, get the scones in the oven as soon as possible. Do the next steps quickly.

Step 9:
Using bare hands, grab a chunk of dough that is roughly 1/3 cup and place chunk onto 1 of the parchment paper-lined half-sheet pans so that 4-6 dough chunks will fit on each pan with at least 2 inches of uniform spacing.

Step 10:
Repeat Step 9 for all remaining dough. These dough chunks will become scones of approximately 4 inches.

Step 11:
Place the pans side by side into the pre-heated oven, on the middle rack. Bake for 8 minutes.

Step 12:
Rotate pans. Bake for 8 to 12 more minutes. Insert a toothpick straight down into the top of the scone, until approximately in the center, then pulled straight back out to see if any dough is sticking to it or if it is "clean". If not clean, then leave pans in the oven for another minute and check again. Check/Recheck until clean.

Step 13:
Remove the pans and place directly on a wire rack to cool.

Step 14:
Wait 5 minutes, then serve.

Fresh Storage:

Once cooled to room temperature, cover scones with plastic film / wrap or place in a plastic sealable bag and store in the refrigerator. May reheat in the oven on a half-sheet pan uncovered or in a microwave uncovered. Use within 1 week.

Frozen Storage:

Once cooled to room temperature, cover scones with plastic wrap or place in a plastic sealable bag, move to refrigerator until completely cooled, then move to freezer. Remove from freezer and place on countertop to thaw before use. May reheat in the oven on a half-sheet pan uncovered or in a microwave uncovered. May be frozen up to 1 month.

Your Notes:

_____

_____

Shortbread

Ingredients:
1 & 1/2 cups butter, softened
1 cup sugar
1 tsp vanilla
zest of 2 lemons
1/4 tsp salt
3 & 1/2 cups all-purpose flour

Directions:
Step 1:
Preheat the oven to 350 degrees.

Step 2:
In a bowl, add butter and sugar, then stir with a spoon / spatula to combine well.

Step 3:
Add vanilla and zest, then stir with a spoon / spatula to combine well.

Step 4:
Add salt and flour, then stir with a spoon / spatula to combine well.

Step 5:
Cover bowl in plastic wrap / film, then transfer to refrigerator to let chill for 30 minutes.

Step 6:
Apply all-purpose flour dusting to the countertop.

Step 7:
Transfer dough to floured surface.

Step 8:
With a rolling pin, roll dough until uniformly 1/2 inch thick square / rectangle.

Step 9:
Using a bench scraper / table knife, cut out a 2 inch square.

Step 10:
Transfer the square to a half-sheet pan.

Step 11:
Repeat Step 9 to Step 10, until all the dough has been cut into squares. Leave a uniform 1 inch spacing between squares on the pan.

Step 12:
Place the pan into the pre-heated oven, on the middle rack. Bake for 20 to 25 minutes, until golden-brown on tops.

Step 13:
Remove pan from the oven and place on a wire cooling rack for 10 minutes.

Step 14:
With a spatula, transfer shortbread squares to serving dishes and serve warm or at room temperature.

This is the perfect way to accompany your morning tea or coffee. Shortbreads can be eaten plain or topped with fresh fruit or marmalade and a side of clotted cream.

Fresh Storage:
Once cooled 10 minutes on the pan, place shortbreads in a plastic sealable bag and store on the countertop for up to 3 days **Or** store in the refrigerator and use within 1 week. May reheat in the oven on a half-sheet pan uncovered or in a microwave on a microwave-safe plate uncovered.

Frozen Storage:
Once cooled 10 minutes on the pan, place shortbreads in a plastic sealable bag, move to refrigerator until completely cooled, then move to freezer. Remove from freezer and place on countertop to thaw before use. May be frozen up to 1 month. May reheat in the oven on a half-sheet pan uncovered or in a microwave on a microwave-safe plate uncovered.

Your Notes:

_____

_____

Soda Bread

Ingredients:
3 cups all-purpose flour
1 Tbsp baking powder
1/3 cup sugar
1 tsp salt
1 tsp baking soda
1 egg, whisked
2 cups buttermilk
1/4 cup butter, melted

This recipe is a quick one. It is important to have everything measured and ready to use before you begin mixing. Your reward will be a hearty bread with a hops flavor "finish".

Directions:
Step 1:
Preheat oven to 325 degrees.

Step 2:
Lightly coat inside of 5 x 9 with non-stick cooking vegetable oil spray. Set aside.

Step 3:
In a bowl, add bread flour, baking powder, sugar, salt, and baking soda, then whisk to combine well.

Step 4:
Add egg, buttermilk, and butter, then stir with a spoon / spatula, until it becomes a uniform mixture. You do not need to knead this bread - quick and easy!

Step 5:
Transfer dough to 5 x 9 inch pan by pouring the mixture then scraping the sides of the bowl with a spoon / spatula.

Step 6:
Smooth the top of the dough with a spoon / spatula.

Step 7:
Place the pan into the pre-heated oven, on the middle rack. Bake for 65 to 70 minutes, until top is golden-brown on top and middle of loaf registers 180 degrees on your thermometer.

Step 8:
Remove pan from the oven and hold upside down over countertop to remove the breads from the pans. **Or** if the bread sticks to the pan, then stick a table-knife straight down between the edge of the pan and the bread, then "run" the knife along all the edges to trace the outline of the bread away from the pan, then hold the pan upside down again to remove the bread from the pan.

Step 9:
Transfer bread onto a wire rack, "right side" side up.

Step 10:
Wait 10 minutes, then slice and serve.

Fresh Storage:

Once cooled to room temperature, cover bread with plastic film / wrap or place in a plastic sealable bag and store in the refrigerator. Use within 1 week. Do not reheat.

Frozen Storage:

Once cooled to room temperature, cover bread with plastic wrap or place in a plastic sealable bag, move to refrigerator until completely cooled, then move to freezer. Remove from freezer and place on countertop to thaw before use. May be frozen up to 1 month. Do not reheat.

Your Notes:

_____

_____

Tortillas

Ingredients:
2 cups all-purpose flour
1/2 tsp salt
1/2 tsp baking powder
1/8 cup butter, softened
1/8 cup lard or solid vegetable shortening / "Crisco"
3/4 cup water (80 to 100 degrees)

Directions:
Step 1:
In a bowl, add flour, salt, baking powder, butter, and shortening. With bare hands, coat shortening and butter a little bit with dry mixture, then begin breaking up shortening and butter with a motion similar to snapping your fingers with your thumb moving across all fingers, while you mix the shortening and butter more with the dry mixture, until the dough is mealy and gritty in appearance and texture (no pieces bigger than pea-sized). Rub hands together to remove any mix that sticks to them.

Step 2:
Add water, then mix with a spoon / spatula to combine. Dough should be slightly moist but not very sticky. If dough is too dry, add 1 teaspoon of water and mix. Repeat this additional water and mixing until the dough is correct. Set aside.

Step 3:
Apply flour dusting to the countertop. Transfer dough to countertop. Cut dough in half. Then, cut each half into half again. Then, cut each quarter in half again, for a total of 8 pieces of dough.

Step 4:
Preheat a large, dry pan on medium heat.

Step 5:
Set out a dinner-size plate or serving platter. Wet a clean dish- / kitchen-towel with warm tap water, wring it out, then place it over the plate / platter.

Step 6:
For each of the 8 pieces of dough, cup your hand over the top of the dough, then roll it around in tight circles on the countertop, to shape it into a smooth and round ball. Set aside until 8 pieces have been made into balls.

Step 7:
On the floured countertop, with a rolling pin, roll out 1 ball into an 8 inch circle.

Step 8:
Lightly spritz hot pan with non-stick cooking vegetable oil spray, then transfer 1 dough circle to the pan, gently lowering it on 1 edge and then laying dough down flat. Fry for 1 minute. You will see the dough begin to bubble: this is a good sign. Using tongs, grasp 1 edge and flip over the dough circle. Fry 1 more minute.

Step 9:
Then, using tongs, grasp 1 edge, hold the tortilla above the pan to allow oil to drain for a few seconds, and then stack on a plain plate or serving platter, covering the tortilla with the warm, damp towel.

Step 10:
Repeat Step 7 to Step 9 until all 8 tortillas have been made. Continue to spritz oil before each dough circle goes into the hot pan. Continue to stack and cover tortillas with the warm, damp towel until ready to serve.

Fresh Storage:
Once cooled to room temperature, cover the tortillas with plastic film / wrap or place in a plastic sealable bag and store in the refrigerator. May reheat in the microwave if spritzed with plain water to avoid over-drying. Use within 1 week.

Frozen Storage:
Do not freeze.

Your Notes:

_____

_____

Bonus Recipes!!!

For bread in danger of becoming stale,

use these recipes to be a bread hero,

or just use the fresh-baked bread

to make an awesome recipe!

Bread Pudding

Can be used for any of the "white" breads and rolls such as Pullman loaves, Challah, dinner rolls, Ciabatta, etc.

Ingredients:
4 cups bread, torn into 1 inch pieces
2 cups heavy cream
1/2 cup milk
1 Tbsp vanilla extract
2 eggs, whisked
1/2 cup sugar

Optional Sauce:
1/2 cup heavy cream
2 Tbsp sugar
2 tsp vanilla
In a pot, medium-low heat, add heavy cream and sugar, then stir frequently with a spoon / spatula for 5 minutes. Remove pot from heat and transfer to a heat-safe surface. Add vanilla, then stir with a spoon / spatula to combine well. Use in Step 6 & 3/4.

Directions:
Step 1:
Preheat oven to 350 degrees.

Step 2:
Lightly coat 8 x 8 inch baking pan with non-stick cooking vegetable oil spray. Set aside.

Step 3:
In a bowl, combine all ingredients, then stir with a spoon / spatula to combine well.

Step 4:
Transfer mixture to pan, scraping bowl to remove all of it.

Step 5:
Place the pan into the pre-heated oven, on the middle rack. Bake for 40 to 45 minutes, until liquids "set" into a pudding.

Step 6:
Remove the pan from the oven, and transfer to a wire rack to cool.

Step 6 & 3/4:
Pour sauce over bread pudding.

Step 7:
Wait 10 minutes, then serve.

Fresh Storage:
Once cooled to room temperature, cover pan with plastic wrap / film and store in the refrigerator. May reheat in the oven in the pan uncovered or in a microwave-safe pan uncovered. Use within 1 week.

Frozen Storage:
Once cooled to room temperature, cover pan with plastic wrap / film, move to refrigerator until completely cooled, then move to freezer. Remove from freezer and place on countertop to thaw before use. May reheat in the oven in the pan uncovered or in a microwave-safe pan uncovered. May be frozen up to 1 month.

Variations:

Banana Rum:
Replace regular vanilla with 2 Tbsp of Rum Vanilla (I make and sell this via my www.twobearschocolates.com site, so message me for inventory and pricing.) Add 2 ripe bananas, mashed and broken into little pieces.

Blueberry:
After stirring all other ingredients, add 1 cup blueberries, then stir gently to combine.

Blackberry:
After stirring all other ingredients, add 1 cup blackberries, then stir gently to combine.

Strawberry:
After stirring all other ingredients, add 1 cup sliced strawberries, then stir gently to combine.

Raspberry:
After stirring all other ingredients, add 1 cup raspberries, then stir gently to combine.

Your Notes:

_____

_____

Croutons

Can be used for any of the "non-dessert" breads or rolls.

Ingredients:
5 cups bread, cut into 1 inch cubes
1/4 cup olive oil
4 tsp garlic, minced
1 Tbsp salt
1/2 tsp fresh ground black pepper

Variations:
Dried herb of your choice (rosemary, oregano, etc)
Add in Step 6 & 3/4.

Directions:
Step 1:
Preheat oven to 350 degrees.

Step 2:
In a bowl, add bread cubes. Set aside.

Step 3:
In another bowl, add olive oil, garlic, salt, and pepper, then stir with a spoon / spatula to combine well.

Step 4:
Drizzle this mixture over bread cubes, scraping the bowl to remove all of the mixture.

Step 5:
Toss with a spoon / spatula to evenly coat the bread cubes with the mixture.

Step 6:
Taste a bread cube. Is there enough garlic, salt, and pepper for your personal taste? If not, then add a little more and toss again to disperse evenly.

Step 6 & 3/4:
Add your choice of dried herb, 1 tsp at a time, until the desired taste is achieved, tossing again to disperse evenly.

Step 7:
Spread the coated bread cubes onto a half-sheet pan.

Step 8:
Place the pan into the pre-heated oven, on the middle rack. Bake for 30 to 40 minutes, until golden-brown on top. Open the oven every 10 minutes to stir and turn over cubes.

Step 9:
Remove the pan from the oven and place pan on a wire rack.

Step 10:
Wait 10 minutes, then serve on salads.

Fresh Storage:
Once cooled to room temperature, place in plastic sealable bag or container and store at room temperature. Use within 5 days.

Your Notes:

_____

_____

Sage Stuffing

Can be used for any of the "non-dessert" breads or rolls.

Ingredients:
8 cups bread torn into 1 inch cubes
2 Tbsp fresh sage, stems removed then finely chopped
1 tsp salt
1/2 tsp fresh ground black pepper
1/2 cup butter
1 medium yellow onion, finely chopped
1 cup button mushrooms, chopped
1/2 cup celery, finely chopped
2 eggs, whisked
1 /2 cup chicken stock / broth
1/4 cup heavy cream

Directions:
Step 1:
Preheat oven to 325 degrees.

Step 2:
Lightly coat a 9 x 13 inch baking pan with non-stick cooking vegetable oil spray. Set aside.

Step 3:
In a bowl, add bread, sage, salt, and pepper, then stir with a spoon / spatula to combine well. Set aside.

Step 4:
In a pan, on medium heat, add butter, then wait until melted.

Step 5:
Add onions, then stir with a spoon / spatula to combine well. Cook for 8 minutes.

Step 6:
Add mushrooms and celery, then stir with a spoon / spatula to combine well. Cook for 8 more minutes.

Step 7:
Transfer pan mixture to bread mixture, then stir with a spoon / spatula to combine well.

Step 8:
Add eggs, stock, and cream, then stir with a spoon / spatula to combine well.

Step 9:
Pour stuffing mixture into pan and cover with aluminum foil.

Step 10:
Place the pan into the pre-heated oven, on the middle rack. Bake for 30 minutes.

Step 11:
Remove the aluminum foil, then bake for another 30 minutes uncovered.

Step 9:
Remove the pan from the oven and place pan on a wire rack.

Step 10:
Wait 10 minutes, then serve.

Fresh Storage:
Once cooled, cover pan with plastic wrap / film and store in the refrigerator and use within 5 days. May reheat in the oven in the pan uncovered or in a microwave on a microwave-safe plate uncovered.

Frozen Storage:
Do not freeze.

Your Notes:

_____

_____

A Bread Poem By James Shipley:

Honey bread is rising in the kitchen
yeast builds airy empires within
Even the Queen would be proud
of this ode to nectar
Flash of heat, barely a chapter
until it is revealed
Tender crumb
melting the honey butter
Explaining the life of bees

Final Words on Bread: A Beginners Guide

My hope is that this book will teach you to start feeling bread texture and to understand when the bread tells you it is ready for the next step. Bread-baking is almost a lost art, and whether you are interested in making bread for special occasions or for everyday use, you are now a part of a resurgence of people who yearn for knowledge that was given up because professional style bread making was just too much of a task for busy people at home. As we consumers continue our journey for finding the easier and faster way of doing things, let us not forget that "better" should be part of that list. Bread-baking is one way to take control of what you are eating, and this guide will help you to make better bread, easier and faster, to accommodate your lifestyle. Enjoy the bread awesomeness journey and have fun!

Chef James Shipley

Made in the USA
Charleston, SC
17 April 2013